# 100 Novel Ways with Book Reports

**Isabelle M. Decker**  Former English Teacher
Oneida (New York) High School

Citation Press, New York • 1969

*Designed by June Martin*

Library of Congress Catalog Card Number: 71-86565

Printed in the U.S.A.

*To*
*CF who first suggested the idea for*
*this book and to RG and CV who gave*
*their constant encouragement.*

# Contents

# By Way of Introduction

Book reports can be a versatile, multi-faceted device to encourage reading, to develop critical thinking, and to stimulate creativity. Unfortunately the potentials are unrecognized and unappreciated by many teachers. In too many instances the book report is a dull, repetitive exercise, an unimaginative name-of-the-book-author-why-you-like-it assignment with no real purpose other than to assure the teacher that the reading has been completed. With such shallow motivation, it is small wonder that students regard the book report with distaste and boredom. To change this image, to encourage practical innovations, to suggest some creative methods and materials, and to induce teachers to reexamine and revise this important aspect of all English courses were the challenges that inspired and instigated the writing of *100 Novel Ways with Book Reports.*

The premise underlying these activities is that the reading itself, not the report, is of prime importance. Students are communicative beings eager to share ideas. Concepts and information gained from their reading can easily be channeled to develop written and oral skills that will foster analytical and critical thinking, essential tools for a lifetime of learning. Activities include all forms of written composition together with a variety of oral presentations to give both the teacher and students many interesting ways to communicate and express themselves. Admittedly novelty has been emphasized, for interest must be aroused before it can be directed. Variety brings freshness and enthusiasm to a standard assignment of the English class that will help eradicate old prejudices against the book report. The activities suggested here are all based on sound teaching principles and techniques that have proved practical and successful when employed wisely.

Since students differ greatly in ambition, specific needs, and especially native ability, a wide variety of activities has been provided to motivate reading with realistic, practical incentives. Frequently changing the format of the book report as well as its subject content, classroom setting, and ways of involving students will help maintain interest. For any of these activities to be effective, however, a teacher must take care to match them to the interests and abilities of his particular students.

Prospective teachers faced with student teaching assignments will find in this book many practical suggestions to sustain them in their insecurity; new teachers, short on tested methods, will appreciate these aids in getting students involved; experienced teachers can replenish and renew ideas to replace those grown stale through repetitious use; department chairmen can use it in counseling teachers. It is the students, however, who will profit most from the variety and novelty of these activities, which make reading a meaningful and satisfying experience. The term "book report" has intentionally been avoided wherever possible; instead the post-reading activities are identified with specific words such as critiques, debates, symposiums, forums, research papers, mini-lectures, and critical analyses, all exact descriptions of the requirements involved. Perhaps if these specific nomenclatures were adopted by the teachers using these activities, a new image could be created with current generations of students, and the old inadequate term "book report" would be banished for all time!

*100 Novel Ways with Book Reports* is not intended to be the cure-all for the doldrums found in some English classes, but it can help stimulate interest in reading while developing written and oral communication abilities. "I like to read, but, oh, how I hate those book reports!" was the plaintive seventh-grade lad's comment that sparked the notion that maybe there *was* a better way with book reports, and hopefully there *are* better ways—in fact, *100 Novel Ways with Book Reports*.

ISABELLE M. DECKER
*Oneida, New York*
*January, 1969*

# 100 Novel Ways with Book Reports

# 1 Roll the Presses

After students have read novels for pleasure, each writes and edits the front page or more of a newspaper that might have been published in the era, city, village, or country in which his novel took place. He includes news items, human interest stories, letters to the editor, editorials, feature columns and departments, advertisements, and even birth and obituary notices based on the locale, personalities, and events of his reading. Because very few novels span a day or a week, he may have to telescope the time elements of some events. By putting himself into their world as the editor of their newspaper, he discovers that he must not only be familiar with his book's plot but knowledgeable about its people and their relationships.

Large pads of press sketching paper are available in art supply stores, and students can paste their typed or lettered columns onto these sheets to resemble a newspaper format. They may have to investigate the nature of journalistic writing or be told about it by their teacher. In cases where the novel was set in a period before newspapers existed, students will have to imagine what a front page would have been like.

This project affords an excellent opportunity to climax a unit on the newspaper with a practical exercise in which an "editor" can apply his imagination freely. The completed newspaper pages make fine display materials. A class newspaper that is published monthly, with a new staff serving for each edition, might develop from this activity.

# 2 Fitting the Review to the Reader

High school students can benefit from a study of the similarities and differences of many types of magazines—literary, juvenile, news, general or family, men's or women's, sports, special interest, organizational, professional, or technical. Everyone in the class selects three types of magazines for detailed study and then, using a supplementary reading book, writes three reviews, each of which is directed to the editor of the book review column or department of the magazines studied. Even if the magazine does not currently have a book review feature, it can be assumed that occasionally it uses this type of material.

Each type of magazine appeals to specific kinds of readers, ages, education or training, personalities, and intelligence, and the book review must satisfy these interests. Each review will therefore differ in content and emphasis and must be an honest appraisal of the book with variations in vocabulary and style.

This activity can serve as part of a regular class unit on magazine writing and appreciation.

# 3 Biographies in Sound

Drawing upon a biography or autobiography he has read, each student writes a radio script in which he presents the background, character, achievements, failures, friendships, philosophy, or other facets of the personality. The script should not be mere narration by an announcer; instead the narration should weave together the voices of friends, enemies, or members of the family who speak in the first person about the biographee as they knew him, influenced him, or were affected by him.

If a student prefers, he can write a dramatization based upon the biography. If additional sources are necessary to round out the material about the subject, they should be consulted. Thus some students may be subtly induced to do additional reading.

The best scripts may be read, with students or teachers serving as the actors. They can also be taped for playback in the classroom or broadcast taped or live over the public address system for several English classes meeting during the same period.

# 4 Shakespeare on Stage

After reading a Shakespearean play, each student can assume the role of a director and plan the staging of the drama in the original Globe Theater, proceeding in the following fashion:

1. Prepare a freehand or traced and labeled drawing of the stage, both front view and floor plan.

2. Divide a sheet of paper into two vertical columns separated by a red line. Use the right column to identify the act and scene by number and to record the required properties or special bits of scenery. Use the left column to state the location of the action, keeping in mind the continuous flow of the action and the numbers of people to be accommodated.

3. List each character and write brief directions for the makeup staff such as, "Ophelia — youthful, beautiful, but pale and disheveled in mad scene" and "King — heavy, well-trimmed beard, ruddy complexion, bushy eyebrows."

4. Using reference books, costume-design books, and other sources, trace or sketch suggested costumes for each of five principal characters.

Students will become so engaged in the creative details of this work that they will not realize they have read and studied the play with greater observation and perception.

As a follow-up to this activity, several scenes can actually be directed and performed by talented students employing scripts and simple costumes and properties. Some of the hilariously humorous scenes can be effective in dispelling lingering doubts among some students that Shakespeare is solely for the sophisticated theatergoer.

# 5 Out of the Mouths of Puppets

Puppets and marionettes have always been part of the theater, and they can be utilized as a creative, dramatic means for presenting book reviews.

A single puppeteer can give a solo performance, controlling one character with each hand and suggesting different voices by changes in volume, voice quality, tone, and rate. He may follow a script posted backstage or tape it beforehand, including sound effects.

Two or three students who have all read the same book may cooperate on writing a script, creating the puppets and stage, manipulating the little characters, and delivering the dialogue. Each can write an initial script, and the best from each can be combined in a joint effort. Reticent students often find great satisfaction in this activity, both from working with others in the writing and in losing their identities in the puppets. Narration is frequently helpful to account for the passage of time and to provide necessary background.

A larger group of students can plan in a committee meeting whether to use one chapter or a collection of scenes and events from their book. After each participant has drawn up an outline for the proposed script, the best ideas are combined and rewritten by one student or jointly. Perhaps two students can work on the writing while the others work out the sets, the staging, the prop list, and the sound or musical effects. After experimenting, they may divide the dialogue, using the most appropriate voices for each character. Much practice is needed to fit the action to the dialogue.

What type of reading is appropriate for a puppet show book report? Almost any type — a scene from a Shakespearean play, one act from a three-act drama, a short story rewritten as a play, a scene from a novel, or material from a travel book. Other possibilities include having two or more puppets discuss a book they have read, engaging in humorous, exaggerated gestures and reactions when they disagree, or having several puppets hold a panel discussion or debate on one or several similar books.

Students may need some information about the various kinds of puppets and how to make them. Simple hand puppets can be made from stockings with flat cardboard heads that are painted with oversized features so they will project to the back of the audience. Hand puppets with hollow rubber balls for heads can be embellished with elaborate putty or clay noses and eyes and mouths cut from construction paper, topped off with frayed rope, string, or paper hair and headgear fastened on with elastic for quick costume changes.

A simple puppet cut out of heavy cardboard and painted and costumed with poster paints is manipulated by attaching a loop large enough for the hand. Although the body movements of these puppets are limited, they appeal to younger students and can be manipulated to make large body movements required by the script. Shadow puppets can be made from distinctive, exaggerated cardboard outlines mounted on a stick one to two feet long, with movable arms attached to smaller auxiliary sticks. A taut white cloth screen is lighted from the rear in a darkened room, and when the puppets are moved behind the screen, they show up black. Properties such as trees, houses, and furniture can be similarly outlined, mounted on sticks, and held in place when needed.

More detailed puppet heads can be made by placing modeling clay on heavy cardboard and forming exaggerated facial features. Strips of paper towels, half an inch wide and dipped into a mixture of flour, salt, and water or wallpaper paste, are laid over the entire mold in layers and the wet paper is pressed into the crevices and indentations. The back of the head is formed with additional clay and covered with wet toweling. After both sections have dried thoroughly, the clay is carefully scraped out, the two sections glued together, the face painted, and hair attached. The neck edge is sewn to a costume suitable for a hand puppet. An index finger inserted into the hollow head permits realistic manipulation.

String marionettes made from wood and hinged together loosely with strips of heavy cloth or leather are more complicated to make and handle, but many books give instructions on their construction, stringing, and manipulation.

Some students may wish to investigate the Chinese form of puppetry in which the puppeteer wears a long, loose black robe and stands in full view of the audience manipulating his string marionettes while delivering the dialogue.

Workable stages have been constructed from large cardboard furniture packing boxes. No floor is needed in the stage for hand or stick puppets, but marionettes manipulated from above require a platform with working space above the stage. A folding stage of some light durable material might be built with the aid of the school's industrial arts department.

If possible, puppets should be kept for reuse by other students for presenting book reviews in this entertaining manner. Changes in costume, of course, may be required.

# 6 Triple Treatment

According to his personal interests and talents, each student chooses a general subject such as aviation, space, war, art, politics, medicine, theater, social problems, psychology, or diplomacy. With the aid of his teacher, the public and school libraries, and catalogs of paperbacks, he plans a reading program that includes novels, biographies, nonfiction, drama, short stories, magazine articles, essays, and poetry. The teacher determines the limits of the assignment according to the age and ability levels of the class and decides whether it will encompass one marking period or one semester.

At the conclusion of the reading period, each student selects one of the following projects:

1. A research paper or 10 to 15-minute speech that is a comparative analysis of the manner in which the same sub-

ject was treated by different styles and forms of literature as well as the effectiveness of each form. If a speech is prepared, it can be taped and submitted to the teacher, and outstanding talks can be played to the class.

2. A four-page brochure supposedly published for a limited group of specialists in the field. Each of the items read is treated separately for its importance and implications to those involved in the field.

3. Students who read about the same subject cooperate in presenting a 30 to 45-minute forum using any plan for content agreed upon by the group.

Students who see no value in supplementary reading and therefore neglect it may realize from this assignment the rewards of gaining new insights and ideas by reading in a field in which they are personally interested. The reluctant reader who will not read, even for pleasure, may be lured into a project if the subject chosen is within his comprehension and interest.

A variation of this activity is to concentrate on one form of literature such as the novel, preferably with additional limitations such as the American novel, the New England novel, or the 19th-century novel. This plan is especially beneficial if a teacher discovers that a class in general suffers from a dearth of reading in a particular literary form.

# 7 I'm a Character

Impersonating one of the characters in a book he has read, each student presents a first person review of some of the most interesting experiences that happened to him in the volume. Travel, biography, novels, and nonfiction are possible choices. The character may disagree with the author of a work of fiction about his fate or the directions his life took. This imaginative, stimulating, and sometimes humorous report can be enhanced, especially in classes where entertainment may be desirable, by wearing a costume or some suggestion of one such as a cape, hat, or robe. Most schools have a costume wardrobe for dramatic activities from which costumes may be borrowed.

This is an excellent activity for national or local book or library weeks, and some of the outstanding performances can be presented at English or literary club meetings or during visitors' day or PTA night.

# 8 Character Building

Using a biography or novel completed for a supplementary reading assignment, each student gives an oral presentation or writes a critique on the theme "Character is nurtured midst the tempests of the world." By example, illustration, evaluation, analysis, or argument he refers specifically to the book's plot, characters, and situations to show how the events and the people involved proved or disproved the truth of the quotation.

Success with this activity may require the teacher to give a preliminary lesson on how to analyze and evaluate composition. Examples from textbooks can be studied with the aid of an overhead projector.

# 9 TV Special

After reading a three- or five-act play, each student writes a script condensing the action of the drama into an hour-long program for educational television. By watching several TV plays critically and examining such books as *Best Television Plays* by Gore Vidal (Ballantine) or *TV Writing* by George Lowther (Collier) students can pick up the techniques. However, they may wish to hold a short period of discussion to pool their observations before writing their scripts.

They can record stage directions, suggested gestures, and camera directions in a three-inch margin on the left side of the paper. For simplicity and uniformity, everyone should assume that three cameras will be used: number 1 for close-ups, number 2 for medium shots, and number 3 for distance or group shots. Instructions for music and sound effects also appear in the left margin. Each script should be accompanied by floor plans for the basic sets. If two students have read the same play, they can cooperate in the writing.

If the school has a closed circuit television system, the best script can be produced and telecast to other English classes; if not, it can be presented on a stage, and the audience can pretend it is in a television studio watching a program being taped. Fake cameras can be created by boys or girls whose scripts may have been duds but who are inventive mechanically. This opportunity to participate will offset their failures in writing and include even the most inept writers in the final activity. All acceptable scripts should be typed, bound in a hard-cover notebook, and placed in the classroom library to inspire others who want to write for television.

# 10 On Stage

After students have read an assigned number of short stories from various sources including current magazines, they choose one to rewrite as a play. They examine published plays to learn the methods of listing the characters, describing the setting, and indicating stage directions. The three best scripts can be presented in walk-through performances in which the actors read the script but are familiar with the lines and the action. The authors will have an interesting reaction watching their plays come to life under the direction of directors they have chosen. Some stories can be staged in pantomime form with a reader or narrator carrying the burden of the lines while the actors perform the action silently.

# 11 Interview Time

After reading biographies, novels, or nonfiction, each student is assigned to be an interviewer and later an interviewee. The interviewer is not told the title of the book read by the classmate he interviews, but he is told the type of literature, the literary period to which it belongs, the nationality of the author, and perhaps additional general information. He composes fifteen questions based on this information and its extensions to the book. Lack of knowledge of the specific title and author prevents his personal prejudices from influencing his questions.

The interview is conducted at a small table in front of the class. A copy of the book is displayed, and the interviewee may quote from it to answer questions. The same students do not work together for the reverse interview because it would tend to follow too similar a pattern; instead, the former interviewer is quizzed by a different student.

The teacher will want to illustrate poor and good types of questions before the interview sessions take place. For example, a poor question is "What is the author's style of writing?" Better questions are "Does the author have a characteristic way of expressing himself? How would you describe it? Illustrate from the book. Why is this style especially appropriate for this volume?"

Students enjoy listening to tapes made from these sessions. The best interviews can be played to classes of lesser ability who seldom hear successful oral work or perceptive analyses of reading experiences. The level of their work can be raised by this exposure, as many poorer students can imitate but not originate.

The value of the book interview for both participants lies in the need for careful reading to be prepared to answer unexpected questions and the necessity of formulating questions that require in-depth answers. Both the interviewer and the interviewee experience a practical and stimulating exchange of ideas as they communicate with each other and the listening audience.

# 12 Three Dimensions

Each student prepares a three-dimensional, diorama-type representation of the theme, locale, characters, plot, era, or other aspect of a book he has read. Somewhere in or on the project he includes a 75-100-word recommendation written in a pithy, direct style. A sea story, for example, may be depicted by a boat tossing on the waves of a wild sea created from a flour, salt, and water mixture that, after it has hardened, is painted with watercolors or poster paint. The recommendation can be placed on a flat area at the front or on the sky background but not on the billowing sails where it would be difficult to read. The title and author must be highlighted to attract attention.

Shoe box replicas portraying scenes from books are also effective and can serve as stage sets for dramas with a workable scale of one-fourth inch per foot. They can be furnished with chairs and tables carved from soft soap. The marquee or stage apron can carry the recommendation.

The teacher will want to specify minimum and, especially, maximum sizes so that he will not be inundated with oversized projects. Book Week or similar occasions provide an opportunity for school-wide display of these projects in the study hall, classrooms, hall display cases, or in specific departments if a book is applicable — science, for example. To keep the activity within bounds, all classes cannot work on it at the same time, and some staggered arrangement is suggested such as one class in October, a second class in November, and a third class in December.

Younger students through the tenth grade are usually enthusiastic about this creative report as is the less able upperclassman who appreciates a de-emphasis on a written report. High ability upperclassmen find such projects boring and prefer a more challenging assignment such as designing a mural based on a nonfiction book or historical novel and writing a 200-300-word description relating the design to the book. The two best murals could be worked out to full size and mounted on the wall of an English classroom, cafeteria, or other suitable place.

27

# 13 Writing for Publication

Writing for publication requires special talents and techniques. Teachers who have had journalism or writing courses or experience writing for newspapers, magazines, or book publishers will be well qualified to carry out this activity, but other teachers can educate themselves by studying textbooks used in schools of journalism and recognized authorities on writing techniques and style. A variety of publications written and produced for use within the school can be a useful outgrowth of a reading assignment.

Divide the class into small committees according to the personal interests of the students and tell each group that it is responsible for publishing a brochure to be either mimeographed or printed by a class in the school's print shop if there is one in the vocational or industrial arts department. These brochures might be for the Science Club, the Conservation Club, the Chess Club, the student government, or similar school organizations. Here are some specific possibilities:

1. The Masquers, the school's dramatic club, needs a brochure to distribute to new members to acquaint them with thé books in the school library that deal with staging techniques, scenery, lighting, directing, costuming, makeup, the history of the theater, past and present, and some of its great personalities. The staff for this brochure can skim and read as many books as is practical and then write brief, informative reviews, which will later be edited.

2. The art or music teacher may need a brochure to distribute to his art or music history and appreciation classes on the outstanding art or music books in the library. The staff of the brochure skims and reads the books, reviews them in good

journalistic style, and contributes its brochure to the art or music departments.

3. Most schools issue a booklet of rules and regulations to incoming classes and transfer students. The guidance department may feel the need for an additional brochure about self-improvement and personal aids available in the school library. A committee can produce a booklet containing reviews of books on personality problems or development, better methods of study, how to prepare for college, how to prepare for college boards and similar examinations, source books listing scholarship opportunities, and volumes considering the social, personal, and emotional problems of teenagers. These brochures can be distributed in homerooms or English classes, or guidance counselors can give them out during conferences with students.

# **14** Posters! Posters!

Each student designs a poster to promote the reading of his book by combining a strategically placed 100-word review with illustrations, lettering, effective arrangement, and other eye-catching details. A discussion of advertising and selling techniques as well as propaganda methods in general should precede this activity. Creating posters can be therapeutic for classes that have a hard-core aversion to the book report and need to be convinced that there are pleasant, painless, and profitable ways to share reading experiences with peers. In the written portions of the posters, students should concentrate on appealing primarily to their associates rather than adults. Displaying these posters throughout the year in class-rooms, halls, the cafeteria, and study halls can be the English department's contribution to the promotion of reading among the student body.

Do any part applicable to the reading:

1. After reading a book about sports, write a brief recommendation, typed or handwritten, on a fairly large cutout of an object involved with the sport featured in the book, e.g., an oversized football, baseball bat, or replica of a football field.

2. Center prominently the title and author of the book and place four significant quotations from the book in boxes at each corner of the poster. A brief recommendation-type review can be placed in the areas not yet utilized.

3. Many books, both fiction and nonfiction, point out that "No man is an island" (Donne). Man's interdependence may be stressed in a summary and recommendation that is mounted upon either a large island cut from a commercial map or an imaginary or actual one created by a student. The theme, "No man is an island," should be prominent. If a student wishes his poster to have multiple pages, the island and the theme could serve as the cover, with the review on the following page or pages, which are also cut to conform with the outlines of the cover page. Other themes with appropriate cutouts could be used with equal effectiveness.

4. A headline "The Critics Say" followed by quotations gleaned from the book's jacket, reviews, or advertisements can be counterbalanced with a headline "And I Say" or "But I Say" followed by a student's recommendation. Illustrations or designs will enhance the effect.

5. Some students are clever at devising crossword puzzles, and a book can serve as the basis for a poster that is a large replica of a crossword puzzle. The "Across" and "Down" listing will appear as is usual, and the puzzle itself will be completed on the poster. A copy of an incomplete puzzle

could be submitted with an answer key to a student magazine or the school newspaper.

6. If students have read biography or travel books, a poster featuring a drawing or replica of an open door or gate, with prominent lettering proclaiming "A Doorway to the World of — " would be suitably symbolic. His review shows how the biography or the travel book introduces a reader into a new world of people or places.

7. A large "C" about five inches high can be drawn at the top center of the poster with the words "As I" placed to the left and the word "it" on the right. The recommendation follows, with illustrations or design to augment the written words. It should be easily read to be effective.

8. After studying weekly book review supplements issued by metropolitan papers, a student can compose a full-page advertisement in the form of a poster to promote his book. The techniques of the commercial artists who design the actual advertisements will suggest ideas, but students should not copy any one arrangement.

9. The words "Absorbing and Timely" are placed at the top of a poster. Some of the chapter headings from a nonfiction book are listed in the upper left section. In the upper right area, a significant quotation from the book appears. Either the title and author or a drawing of a book containing the title and author can be in the center followed by the recommendation keyed to the words "absorbing" and "timely." Additional decoration that is significant may be desired.

10. The subject matter of some books suggests objects such as houses, rockets, cars, trains, castles, or hospitals, and a poster could be a cutout of the object with the report recommendation mounted on it. Edison's biography would be appropriate on a cutout of an electric light bulb, and a biography of a president would be effective on a White House mounting.

11. One of the headline comments listed below can introduce a written recommendation of 75-100 words.

I dare you to read ——— by ———.
Nothing to do? Why not read ——— by ———?
Sick of school and want to get away? Then travel to ——— with ——— in ———.
Take my advice and read ——— by ———.
It's right off the presses! It's different! Read ——— by ———.
Want to improve your ———? Then read ——— by ———.

I liked it. You will too. Read ——— by ———.

The latest slang expression of approbation, if it is popular and in good taste, could also be the lead line for this type of poster.

#  Quotes

After completing assigned supplementary reading, each student peruses a book of quotations in the classroom, school, or home library. Using the index to suggest possibilities, he attempts to find a quotation that is applicable to a character or characters, the plot or some parts of it, the theme and its implications, the locale, or the historical era of his book. Placing the quotation at the top of his paper, he proceeds to write about its relevance to his reading, working from an outline previously submitted to his teacher. General statements should be illustrated with examples, and conclusions should be logically drawn.

An effective way to initiate this activity is to hold a workshop session during which an outline is developed on the blackboard using one student's book and quotation. This can be followed by a writing workshop during which the students write their critiques. The ideas evoked by the quotations will generate new thoughts, and the formerly dull book report will become a tool to teach effective thinking and communication.

# 16 Let's Talk

To launch this activity, spend a class session examining publishers' catalogs of paperback books, current brochures of junior and senior high school book clubs, and copies of the supplements on paperbacks published by *The New York Times* and other metropolitan newspapers. As they look these over, students should note titles they think they would like to read. Lists compiled by students who have looked over the racks of paperbacks in local bookstores are additional helpful sources.

Each row of students or similar small groups within the class structure meet during a class period to select the paperback everyone will read. Their chairmen, who have been selected by lot, lead the sessions and report the choices to the teacher. No two groups should read the same book. The teacher, of course, may prefer to assign a special type of book to each group so that all varieties of reading materials will be covered. The low cost of paperbacks permits every student to have his own copy, thus avoiding the time lag necessary if each student had to wait for the one or two copies in the school library to become available.

After meeting the reading deadline, each group plans a discussion or forum, consulting public-speaking textbooks if necessary to learn procedures and techniques. The chairman is responsible for guiding his group through the planning period and making sure each participant understands how the group will function. After-school planning sessions are best as it is impossible to talk freely when competing with other groups in the same room. The teacher will want to assure the chairmen that, although their primary objective is to keep the discussion moving along constructively, they need not be neutral. They too can and should contribute ideas to stimulate, to irritate, or to otherwise goad those they are leading to express and expand upon their ideas, reactions, and contributions.

The teacher may also suggest on a dittoed sheet a plan of action such as the following:

1. From the readers' points of view, why did the author write this book? Did he have an objective or a message? To achieve this, how did he utilize his characters, the events, or otherwise emphasize the theme? Were his opinions prejudiced or ill founded?

2. If the book is a novel, did the events influence the development of the characters or vice versa? What is the basic plot? Where do the subplots intertwine, if at all? Is the author a slave to plot?

3. What is the outstanding characteristic of the author's writing style? Is it similar to the technique of other writers known to the group? Is the style appropriate for the subject matter? Does it increase the book's impact? Could the style be different and the theme still maintain its effect? Is it easy to read? Is ease of reading necessary to the success of the book? Explain.

4. What was the implication of the ending for the characters, the theme, or for the reader? What is the climax? How important is it? Does the book conclude with the climax? What is the impact of the ending?

5. What is the major appeal of the book, giving specific answers? Is it for popular consumption? Is that important? Was this the author's intent?

6. Did the book add to the readers' knowledge, self-understanding, or group-understanding? If not, where does it fail?
7. If applicable, discuss definitions of a classic. Is this book a classic? How does it meet the specifications? Will it become a classic? Defend opinions.
8. All reading should have some value. Evaluate this book's worth to the individual members of the panel and to the average reader.

This activity offers an ideal opportunity to teach a lesson on the duties and responsibilities of a committee chairman since the information will not be isolated but immediately relevant and applicable. The teacher will probably want to include such advice as:

1. The chairman alerts all members of his group to the specific phases of the discussion for which each is responsible. He records on 3 x 5 inch cards the questions and topics the group has decided to include in the discussion, and each person, including the chairman, prepares answers to the questions.
2. He instructs his committee that answers are not to be written and read but to be given from notes or from memory. He may even schedule a practice session in an empty study hall during the noon hour or after school.
3. He tells each participant to bring his copy of the book with underlined or marked passages to serve as examples during the forum.
4. He abides by the time limitation set by the teacher.
5. During the practice and actual sessions he purposely calls on reluctant members for contributions and opinions and tries to restrain aggressive, talkative members. He can express his own opinions, but must be careful not to dominate the discussion.
6. He identifies the book and the names of the speakers when introductions are needed.

7. When the group has covered all the planned questions or when the time limit has been reached, he may wish to ask the audience for questions or comments. Depending upon the size of the room or the clarity of the questioner, he may have to repeat the question and refer it to a specific participant if the questioner has not done so.

8. Summarizing the discussion is absolutely necessary to leave a strong, positive impression; therefore he may have to take some notes during the discussion to assist him in formulating intelligent, logical conclusions to leave in the minds of the audience.

Discussions such as these can be taped for use in other English classes. Students of lesser ability enjoy such programs as they have an element of entertainment, but more importantly they provide them with some techniques to copy when they are faced with communicating their ideas on their reading. Playing a portion of the tape when parents visit the classroom on visitors' night or during National Education Week will assure them that leadership and communication skill are being taught to their children and, surprisingly, through the book report.

An excellent way to build a classroom library is to suggest that the paperbacks bought for this activity, as well as those purchased from book clubs or for other occasions, be contributed throughout the year on a loan basis. The owner of each book should be identified, and a method of check-out determined and supervised by two student librarians. Throughout the year the books will receive more use than if they were kept in students' personal libraries. At the close of school each student retrieves his contributions or chooses as many books from the collection as he contributed. Some may choose to leave their books as gifts. When students participate in building their class library, they are stimulated to read more because it's their library, not the teacher's.

# 17 Catching Up with the Classics

"Students who are well-grounded in the children's classics do the best work in college English class," the chairman of a college English department once remarked to me.

Working with bibliographies available from the school librarian and the teacher, class members compile their own bibliographies of the best-known children's classics. The final mimeographed bibliography is given to each student and posted on the bulletin board; it should cover short stories, poetry, novels, and travel — all types of books, fact or fantasy! A one-month reading campaign at the upper-grade levels or a three-month period on the seventh-grade level called "Catching Up with Children's Classical Literature" can then be organized because too many students have not read these classics. The teacher may wish to set some goals such as ten pieces of literature for the seventh grade and five pieces for the twelfth grade or, if his philosophy dictates, a reversal of the size of the assignments.

The objective is to encourage students to read as many different selections as possible. Therefore the posted bibliography has spaces to record the names of the students reading the selections, preferably no more than two students to each title. At the conclusion of the reading period, a critical essay in the form of a magazine article that may be printed in a publication for parents should be written by each student. Again the number of words can be scaled for different grade levels.

Taking the theme "Evaluating the Children's Classics," the student develops the subject referring specifically to the books or selections he has read. The teacher may wish to give the class some suggestions such as these for guidelines:

1. What is a children's classic? Begin with the dictionary

definition, progress to the literary experts' opinions, and conclude with the student's ideas.

2. Name five characteristics of children's classics. How does each of the readings illustrate them? Why do the classics maintain their popularity? How or why do they stir the imagination, and is this a necessary characteristic of children's literature?

3. Be sure to include a conclusion that will prompt parents who will read the article to promote this type of reading among the children in their families.

More mature questions can be substituted for older groups.

The ten best articles can be read by students who enjoy oral reading, and a student chairman can lead a discussion of controversial issues raised. In some classes each student might simply tell his classmates about his favorite among the reading he has done. A group of the most able students could develop a program for presentation to a PTA or a school parents' club. Mimeographed, annotated bibliographies would enhance such a program.

A variation is possible by using the outline suggested above. Instead of preparing a magazine article, students can take notes on their reading for a class interchange of ideas — call it a mass dialogue perhaps. This is conducted by a chairman chosen by the class or the teacher for his leadership qualities.

The chairman encourages participation by asking such questions as: "Do you agree with that statement, Joan?" or "Mary, you have a young brother. Is that the reaction he has had to ———?" or "Mark, you contend that children's stories are too fantastic. Then explain the popularity of science fiction." The students' marks can be based on both the card notes and participation in the discussion. A secretary should be appointed to take notes and to prepare a ditto sheet for distribution to the class members for later testing.

A discussion program for public presentation can also be evolved. The teacher can, in the instance of either a classroom or a public performance, interject some spontaneity by giving the chairman new material to which the students have not previously been exposed. If the teacher uses a small discussion group, he can introduce an aura of change by taking the class into the auditorium where panel participants can perform on the stage.

The value of this activity to upper classmen will be greatest with college-bound youngsters who would acquire a foundation for further literary study, terminal groups who face parenthood within the next few years and can use a familiarity with children's literature to guide their family reading, and future librarians and elementary teachers in the class.

# 18 Researching the Novel

To increase his knowledge and appreciation of the novel as a literary form, each student reads at least 50 pages of literary criticism about novels, using indices and tables of contents to locate appropriate commentary in volumes of essays and criticism. He then reads a novel and prepares a five-minute oral analysis of it based on the criteria found in the research material.

Instead of studying the novel form in general, a class can also concentrate on specific categories of novels such as the psychological novel, the journalistic novel, or the protest novel. The teacher can assign appropriate background reading for research periods and then divide the class into equal-size groups, each of which will read novels of one category. Their findings, reactions, recommendations, and knowledge about their literary form can be communicated to their peers in forum or symposium discussions.

# 19  Let's Travel

After reading travel books students pretend they are the authors who have been invited to speak on their travel experiences to a particular group. Each speaker identifies his audience — International Explorers Club, Rotary Club, National Geographic Society, Travel Trailers Association, or Students on Tour Association. Within a set time limit he selects and recounts the episodes and adventures in the book that will have the greatest appeal to his special audience. He may use maps, the blackboard, and other appropriate material, including a costume or part of one, to enhance the presentation. Music on tapes or records that relate to the book can be included, but no slides are to be used.

The teacher can call these talks "A Travel Lecture Series to Be Presented by the Members of the First Period English Class During the Week of ———," and posters on the school bulletin boards can advertise them. Students with free periods can be invited to attend if the series is held in the auditorium or a large lecture room. Students can vote on the best lecture of the series, and some appropriate award based on all-round visual and oral qualities can be given.

# 20 Around the Campfire

Seventh- and eighth-grade students enjoy and crave action both in and out of the classroom. This project capitalizes on their natural interest in books and movies of adventure and their flair for original dramatics. Five or six boys may plan or discover accidentally that they have all read books of an adventuresome nature. They construct or borrow from the dramatics department a campfire of modest size, usually constructed of logs, colored gelatines in yellow and red, and a light bulb. Chairs and desks are moved to the sides of the room for the audience. If the room has fixed desks, this activity can be carried out on a stage with the audience sitting around the edges. Dim lights on the stage give greater reality to the fire, and in the classroom shades can be drawn to enhance the effect.

The participating actors may add three or four sleeping bags and assorted props, such as artificial rocks for leaning and lounging on plus other items their active imaginations will conjure up for the set. As the scene opens, the boys are sprawled in or on the sleeping bags and rocks, with perhaps one fellow providing some soft guitar music or even a camp-type song. The boys who will be reading can use flashlights for illumination, an acceptable camping practice.

The conversation might proceed like this:

FIRST BOY (*slapping his book shut*): Finished! Cool book (or whatever the latest expression of approval is at that moment)!
SECOND BOY (*still strumming guitar*): What is it?
FIRST BOY: (*names the book*)
THIRD BOY: Who wrote it? I always pick my books by the author. I have some favorites like ———. If I pick his books, then I know they'll be keen.
FIRST BOY: This one is by the fellow who climbed Mt. Everest. Remember ———.
FOURTH BOY (*looks up from his whittling*): I looked at that one day in the library. It's long. Good pictures though.
THIRD BOY: Is that the one about ———?
FIRST BOY: Yes, and he also ——— etc.

In this case the boys had all read the same book, but the

same sort of dialogue can be developed if all of them have read different books. Of course, the boys proceed to discuss the book in detail and may offer some profundities, seventh-grade style, on adventure books in general.

A script should not be prepared, but the group will secretly choose a leader, perhaps the lad who inaugurates the conversation, whose job it is to keep the conversation flowing. At a planning session the boys decide the points to be covered, including ways to suggest the value the reading had for them and the appeal it would have for other boys their age.

The teacher should point out that students are not expected to use such stilted conversation as, "What is the author's style of writing, John?" but instead express the same thought in the vernacular: "I liked the way he wrote it. You really feel that you were right there standing beside Malcolm up on the bridge of the ship with the captain during the storm (*searches for the marked page in the book*). Like this "——— (*reads a good example of the author's realism*)".

They might pursue the idea of compulsive reading thus:

FOURTH BOY: It is the kind of book you can't put down until you finish.
FIFTH BOY: I wonder why some books are like that?

The exploration of that idea might lead them to the conclusion that reading must first fit the reader's interest.

When the bell rings, bringing everyone back to reality, it will be hard to convince the class that this period has been devoted to the book report routine they used to hate!

Girls may clamor for equal time to discuss a book or books appropriate to their interests, such as one about a girl whose father is an ambassador to a foreign country and the adventures of family living in an exotic land or biographies about famous women, especially those that concentrate on their youthful years. The same camp setting can be employed, perhaps with some feminine refinements, or girls' ingenuity may create a different setting that is equally effective for natural dialogue.

Older students can employ the same technique. Often three or four students will read the same book or books with a similar theme such as war or a similar genre such as books by American southern authors. To take advantage of this group experience, suggest that they pretend to be in an informal setting such as a favorite local hangout where, supposedly sitting around a table having cokes, they can discuss their books before their classmates. A few posters and subdued lights can create the atmosphere. Another possibility to induce informality and help banish the fears some students have of formal speaking before an audience is to imagine that the participants are working on costumes or scenery for the next Dramatic Club performance. As they work — no hammering, please — they talk about their reading. Two boys in an imaginary shop class could be sanding their latest project as they talk, or the familiar situation of eating lunch in the cafeteria can be utilized. Students themselves will think up other novel settings if the possibility of freedom from the normal classroom formality is offered. De-emphasizing the classroom works wonders in creating an atmosphere conducive to better communication and greater honesty of thought and opinion. If the students are mature, they can consider the latest controversial novel and the problems of censorship, ensuring a rousing discussion that will generate a variety of opinions.

The teacher must impress upon participants that, although their conversation is casual and seemingly impromptu, the group must meet in committee ahead of time to plan the general areas they will explore and the direction the discussion will take. One student should assume the leadership, but he does not promote all the ideas.

# 21 A Grueling Grilling

By prearrangement, four students read the same book. They assume these roles: the author of the book, a literary critic on a magazine, a literary editor of a metropolitan newspaper, and a student who serves as chairman of a symposium presented for high school students of all grade levels.

The chairman introduces the speakers and identifies the book for the audience. The critics quiz the author with a variety of questions, some controversial, to keep the session lively and informative. The student chairman participates in the role of the average reader who wants to understand the author's philosophy and objectives in writing this particular work. Very ambitious students can enrich this experience by reading several of the author's books, which will afford them greater knowledge as well as additional discussion material.

An interesting variation is to permit the student playing the role of the author to become one of the critics. Because of his previous grilling, he can now inject some retaliatory probing that will enliven the discussion. Arranging chairs behind a long table facing the audience lends realism, and boldly printed name cards identifying the participants add formality and dignity.

# 22 Quiz Time

Each student composes an examination based on the book he has read and also prepares an answer key to all the questions. He can include true and false, multiple choice, matching, and some essay questions. In the case of the latter, his answer key contains only an outline of the answer he would expect if he were correcting the exam. The teacher can scale the required number of questions up or down according to the age and ability levels of the class. If another student reads the book later, his report can consist of answering the questions, and the creator of the test can score and mark it. Students engrossed in this assignment see no resemblance to a book report, yet to formulate questions they must read carefully and think through the book and its implications for the reader.

# 23 Questions! Questions!

When two or three students have read the same book — and the teacher might make the assignment with this stipulation — they each prepare ten discussion-type questions about it and submit them to the teacher who spots duplicate ideas and requests substitutions and then selects the 15 most provocative contributions. None of the questions, which are written on separate 3 x 5 inch cards, are revealed to the other participants. On the day of the report, the students sit at a desk or table in front of the class and each in turn takes a card at random and answers the question on it. If a card contains the student's own question, that is all right as it will add to the positive quality of his answer. If an answer does not satisfy the individual who created the question, he can probe for a better answer or augment it with further comments. There is no chairman for this activity; all the participants share the responsibility for its success. At the end of the quiz period the teacher and class members can continue some informal questioning if they feel that clarification or further explanation is necessary. This type of exposure to practical public speaking in which participants are prepared with solid content material builds communication expertise in English classes.

# **24** Who Is It?

After reading biographies or autobiographies, each student writes a biographical sketch of the person but avoids using his name in the 200–300-word summary. The name, however, is recorded at the bottom of the page. The sketches are read during a class session, and the audience tries to guess the identity of each biographee. The sketches should contain more than vital statistics and reveal the events and people who influenced the individual in his friendships, personality growth, achievements, disappointments, and failures. Such a session can introduce students to new people and perhaps subtly suggest that by reading biographies they will gain more understanding of how others met and solved problems.

# **25** Literary Detectives

Each student in upper-class English courses finds in newspapers, magazines, or review media such as the Sunday *New*

*York Times Book Review* and similar metropolitan publications three reviews about the same type of book he has just completed, e.g., novel, biography, or anthology. He clips each review, pastes it in a single column on the left side of a sheet of paper, and draws a line to separate it from the blank right column. He then proceeds to act as a literary detective to discover the outline the review writer must have used to plan and write the criticism. The teacher may wish to elaborate on the need for planning before taking action, drawing parallels from other fields of endeavor.

The student detective reads each review first for enjoyment and information. A second reading should begin to reveal details unnoticed before. Using the generally accepted outline symbols of I., II., III., for main topics, A., B., C., for subtopics, and 1., 2., 3., and a., b., c., for additional subdivisions, he annotates the margins surrounding each review. In the right column he organizes the outline he has discovered in a formal form, e.g., I. Background, II. Main Characters, and III. Plot Events.

He then chooses one of the outlines whose arrangement best fits the subject and material of the book he has read and writes a review of it, adapting the outline to meet his needs. He thus learns from the experts that effective writing adheres to respected rules of organization. Completed outlines can be projected for viewing by the entire class as students read the reviews they have based upon them. The class will be expected to criticize the reviews for their content and for the degree of success the writers achieved in using the second-hand outline.

Because of the amount of work done by the class on this project, the teacher will probably want to preserve the best outlines for future use. Such mimeographed outlines can be employed for writing reviews when students have not been given specific instructions. For example, some of the activities in this book suggest only an oral or written form of report, and students and teachers must supply the content plan. An on-hand supply of outlines would be helpful in such instances.

# 26 Words at Work

Working as a large research group, class members collect book reviews after their teacher has conducted a discussion during which all sources suggested are listed on the board. Specific newspapers, national adult and student magazines, publishers' advertisements, book jackets, and book club advertising pamphlets will be among the many suggestions.

During two class periods students will work individually studying as many reviews as possible with the specific objective of finding and recording in their notebooks clever, effective, and picture- and thought-creating words and phrases that reviewers used to explain, clarify, or interpret the characters, setting, situations, plot development, writing style, or any other aspect of a book. Many of these words and phrases will be unfamiliar to the students, and the teacher will probably recommend the use of dictionaries during these collection sessions. Under the heading "Effective Vocabulary for Book Reviewing," each student compiles, depending on the grade level, 100-200 discoveries. A brief annotation should follow each word or expression explaining its application in the review in which it was found. For example:

> rings true — conversation or dialogue
> bewildering cross currents — events in the plot
> controversial judgments — author
> fortitude — character
> all-inclusive — subject matter

Well organized students might list the words on separate pages labeled with the application such as "Used to Describe Characters" or "Used to Describe Subject Matter." The list must have a variation of applications and not be limited to one aspect such as plot.

Each student then writes a review incorporating 10–15 of the words or expressions as they apply to his book. He underlines the words to identify them, but he need not use them exactly as the original writer employed them. For example, the word "fortitude" may have described a characteristic of the hero, but the student writer may find it more apt to apply it to his author for his courage in writing on a controversial subject.

At first this procedure may seem artificial, but after the first attempt at using more vivid language, students discover that they too have words and phrases that will work for them to make writing more enjoyable. The best way to absorb new vocabulary has long been recognized as immediate use and reuse of a new word; this activity provides such exercise.

# 27 Question and Answer Time

After all students have read books in one subject area such as vocations or space exploration, each composes on separate 3 x 5 inch cards five thoughtful questions applicable to the topic. All types of literature may be read from novels to dramas, but the emphasis will be on nonfiction. The teacher should also contribute ten or more questions to bolster the depth of the questioning and to replace some of the inadequate or repetitive questions that he and a student committee will be forced to remove.

The cards are mixed thoroughly in a box, and each student draws four cards. If he pulls a question he has authored, he exchanges it for another. The teacher, who is familiar with the class and its general ability, must decide whether to give the students one day to prepare oral answers or only a five-minute thought session. If the former, spontaneity is sacrificed to the thoughtfulness of the answers. Students answer only one question at a time, and anyone in the group can challenge an answer or augment it.

The element of playing a game can be introduced by having a panel of judges consisting of the teacher and two elected students or, better yet, two neutral students from another class. Each judge has five fairly large cards each bearing a number from five to one. The class is divided into two or three teams who compete against each other for the largest number of points. When a student answers his question, each judge decides the number of points he feels it is worth and holds up that numbered card. Scoring clerks keep the record for each team. When all the questions have been answered, the teacher may wish to add some bonus questions to be answered by anyone on a team to either break ties or add points. This is a subtle way to introduce material student questions have failed to reveal.

The teacher will recognize that this activity affords the opportunity to teach another phase of composition — the formation of questions that promote thinking. He can make transparencies for the projector depicting good and poor examples. After reading books about animals, for instance, a poor question would be, "What is the animal in your story?" whereas a good multi-faceted question would be, "What is the outstanding characteristic of the animal in your book? Show by example the proof of your statement. Do people ever have this trait? In the same way? Explain." Thus he shows that a question, to be effective, often develops one idea in several stages.

Students may wish to sit in a large circle if no points are

given for answers. They will enjoy hearing the questions they composed answered, even if the responses are quite different from what they expected. For students not yet ready to face an audience to give a book talk, these short-answer experiences provide good training that will move them along gradually into small-group and solo speech situations. This activity also proves that reading experiences can often be shared and that there can be fun and excitement in that experience.

# **28** Dear Pen Pal

Students pretend they have a pen pal in another state and that they have decided to exchange a book for Christmas or some other occasion. To make the gift more meaningful, each reads the book before he sends it to the other and then writes a letter describing his reactions to it feeling free to criticize it in any manner he chooses. His friend in turn writes his impressions of the book after he has received and read it.

A variation is to divide the class evenly into hometowners and out-of-staters. Each student records his name on a card and lists his general and specific reading interests in types of literature and subject areas. If he is a hometowner, he so labels his card, and if he is an out-of-stater, he lists a city and state where he supposedly lives. The latter group of cards are placed in a box, and the hometowners each choose one, and vice versa. Each student, armed with the information he knows about the reading interests of his pen pal, obtains a book from his personal library, the classroom library, or the public library and "sends" it to his friend across the country (the room), first reading or skimming it thoroughly.

He writes a letter to his pal discussing the book and later receives a similar letter. The comparison of ideas will be interesting. Of course, they repeat the process with a second book.

The teacher will want to read from anthologies examples of informative letters written by the great and the not so great. Reading excerpts from novels that were conceived as a series of letters or from memoirs or biographies can also provide new insights for students who may have no concept of the importance of the letter in literature. Some students may even become interested enough to read examples of such books and report back to the class. Three or four pen pal letters that exemplify good letter writing skills and have solid commentary on the books read should be read aloud to give class members models to imitate in the future.

# 29 Successful Salesmen

After students have been informed of the requirements, they select books to read well in advance of the December holidays. The choices are important and must have genuine appeal because each student will be expected to prepare and deliver a sales talk to persuade his listeners that his book would be an excellent gift to give special friends or relatives. He may wish to define the type of person to whom the volume would appeal, perhaps an ill, busy, erudite, sports-minded, or young person. A student chairman supervises the program of talks and distributes to everyone in the audience a dittoed sheet with the following column headings: "Speaker's Name," "Book Title and Author," "Did He 'Sell' the Idea of Purchasing the Book?" and "For Whom Was the Book

Suggested?" At the conclusion of each speech a show of hands will indicate to the speaker how successful a salesman he was.

For this activity to succeed on all grade and ability levels, some introductory study of the techniques and skills of effective salesmanship may be necessary. An attractive bulletin board seems an almost inevitable by-product. For example, book jackets and captions that state the suitability of the volume for various relatives or types of readers can be arranged against a background of a huge gift package.

# 30 Holiday Time

Special holidays during the school year suggest appropriate reading assignments and utilize profitably pre-vacation days that are often frittered away in holiday anticipation. The teacher makes the reading assignment and explains the follow-up activity well in advance, so the reading can be unhurried and the resulting program well prepared. Thanksgiving, the December holidays, and the spring recess suggest a wealth of literature associated with these times of year. If, however, a local school or area objects to the specific implications or actual use of religious material for school programs, an excellent substitute that could cause no difficulties would be a theme such as "World Literature," "Literature from Around the World," "International Literature," or "Literature of East and West." National Brotherhood Week or United Nations Day are suitable times for international literary emphasis.

Each member of the class is expected to contribute at least two suggestions of literature appropriate for or related to the chosen theme or holiday. They need not be complete books but can include essays from anthologies or magazines, short stories, poems, dramas, novelettes, novels, or nonfiction volumes. The title, author, and source must accompany each contribution. A student committee chosen by lot or by the teacher prepares a master list and fills out some of the weak areas for balance. The list is either typed and posted or mimeographed with copies for all, plus one copy for the classroom archives for the use of future students.

After students have read the required number of selections from the list, they write for each title a summary of their reactions in not less than 25 or more than 50 words on 3 x 5 inch cards. Since the selections will vary in length, the assignment will probably be given in terms of the number of pages to be read, and thus some students will contribute more cards than others.

Committee chairmen then work with the teacher to plan a program to be given by and for the class during the two days prior to the vacation. Each committee utilizes the reading report cards to choose the material to be used for different kinds of presentations such as: short selections to be read in their entirety, excerpts from long selections, brief dramatizations from long plays, original dramas created from short stories, summaries of nonfiction material, reviews of books with the reporter dressed as the main character, puppet shows (see Activity 5), pantomime performances with a narrator and actors, formal dramatic readings by one or a group of three or four using stools and music stands, or live music or literature records. The overall format could be a radio program or a TV special.

The performance may be given in a rearranged classroom, a music room, a corner of the cafeteria, or the auditorium. Students and teachers with free periods can be invited to attend to swell the audience. The program might even become a closed circuit TV show or assembly program for the entire student body.

The general chairman will work with greater responsibility if he is called the producer; the master of ceremonies can enjoy prominence as the director, assisted by the technical director for audio-visual arrangements and the stage manager for lights, props, and sets. The teacher, of course, will be the coordinator.

The effectiveness of this activity depends upon the initial reading experiences of the students plus their cooperation in producing a worthwhile program during the days preceding a vacation. For many this will be a first experience in making literature come alive under their own direction and planning.

# 31 Lots of Exhibits

After completing a supplementary nonfiction reading assignment on one theme such as "Travel and Exploration," "Scientific Discoveries," "Heroes of American History," or "Folklore of the World," a survey is taken of the specific books read. Students and teacher work out on the blackboard subdivisions of the overall theme. For example, if the topic was "Adventure," the subdivisions might be Real Life Adventures, Fictitious Adventures, Sea Adventures, Wartime Adventures, Aviation and Space Adventures, Discovery or Exploration Adventures, or Women Adventurers.

The class will divide into small groups according to the reading done. These small committees prepare an exhibit not to exceed the size of two card tables and a bulletin board based on the subject of their subdivision. For Sea Adventures the exhibit might include replicas of ships or scenes suggested by the books, dolls dressed as characters, soap or clay sculptures of sea items, or actual artifacts associated with specific books. The bulletin boards might contain a map, diary entries, pictures, and similar materials. The books can be displayed on the chalk tray beneath the bulletin board or near the exhibit. After arranging the materials, the elected chairman leads the group in a discussion of why the books were exciting or different, what life at sea was like, the elements of suspense, the value of the reading, or other topics suggested by committee members or the teacher. The group might even decide to give a series of short talks on each book, with all members combining in a final question-and-answer period involving the audience.

The display is scratched after one day's showing, and the next subdivision group proceeds in the same way. Because of space limitations, the teacher may wish to restrict this activity to one section of his class.

# **32** On the Map

If the supplementary reading has been about travel or exploration or is a commentary on the people and problems of another country, continent, or area, each student draws an outline map of that geographical entity on notebook or typewriter paper. They cut out the silhouettes and write or type their reports on it and additional identical sheets. If the reports are securely stapled at the tops, they can be displayed on bulletin boards. No covers are to be used as they discourage viewers from reading the reports. The teacher may wish to assign his own guidelines for the written report or to use one of the outlines suggested elsewhere in this book. Sometimes it is wise to assign a broad topic such as "Reading

That Extends Our Horizons" so that in discussing their particular book students can practice their skills in specific application. Whatever the approach, the result should be the same — an opening of eyes and minds to new knowledge and understanding.

# 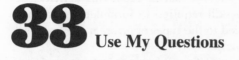 Use My Questions

This is an effective post-reading activity to assign after a class has read various kinds of literature that deal with the same topic such as government and politics, culture in America, democracy, 'isms of the world, emerging nations, Asian affairs, job opportunities in today's business world, the theater of the last 25 years, or any of dozens of other possibilities.

Each student imagines he is a teacher who must create a series of essay questions to be answered by his students in reporting on the books read. The series must cover at least five distinct areas. For example, "Define democracy. Relate briefly your book's association with democracy. Do the author's ideas differ from the generally accepted definition? How does he prove his points?" would be one question.

The real teacher collects all the questions and distributes them to other members of the class for criticism. The student critic will look for vagueness, repetition, or incongruity plus technical errors in spelling, punctuation, or structure. After he has noted his suggestions, he returns the paper to the original student, who then analyzes the comments and attempts a minor or major revision. The teacher then examines the series, adds major or general comments on the back, and redistributes them, taking care not to give the original creator or his critic the questions on which they have worked. Giving the girls' questions to the boys and vice versa might produce interesting results.

An entire period is then turned into a writing workshop during which each student writes a review of his book based on the questions he has received. Since all the books dealt with the same general subject matter, the questions should be adaptable to all the titles. At the end of the period the reports are given to the creators of the original questions, who correct the reviews and suggest marks. From this activity students learn about the skill required to formulate clear questions and are introduced to the types of errors made by themselves and their classmates.

A variation of this activity is to select just one series of questions and distribute dittoed copies to everyone in the class. In this case the criticism and correction phases can be effected by a general exchange of papers.

Some classes may need some preliminary work before attempting this activity. They can learn how to construct good questions if the teacher works out on the board a sample using a subject such as historical fiction. Superior questions, as well as poor examples, can be projected for analysis by the class and teacher. Also the written reports, both good and poor, can be examined in detail. Students plagued by inadequacy in their work need this kind of constructive help, and everyone can be inspired by exposure to excellence.

# 34 People and History

Upperclassmen struggling with difficult courses in history and English often do not have time for supplementary reading for both courses. Occasionally combining assignments permits greater concentration of time and effort and achieves rewarding results. History teachers will appreciate the work of the English teacher in helping students to develop through their reading and writing an understanding of the world and its many complex problems.

With the aid of bibliographies contributed by the school librarian and the history department plus catalogs of paperbacks, class members select a general topic relevant to their history course. One student might also interview some of the history teachers for suggestions. Communism, the emerging nations, American urban problems, social unrest, Near East transitions, or the work of the United Nations are all potential themes. If possible, the reading should not be restricted to nonfiction but include drama, novels, some contemporary poetry, and certainly magazine articles that pertain to any aspect of the subject.

The teacher will probably wish to set limits to the assignment; perhaps he will require reading two choices from the list. Each student will be expected to write a paper of 300–600 words depending on the ability of the group and the length of the assignment. The theme of the paper will be determined by the general subject and the teacher. For example, if the subject is American politics, the theme might be "The Good and Evil Aspects of Politics in America," and the assignment might be "Define politics using textbook and dictionary meanings and your interpretation. On the basis of the characters, events, or other material in your book, explain the climate of the political times. Be specific. Were political upheavals and changes highlighted? Evaluate three political weaknesses of the times. Illustrate. If the book is not concerned with contemporary politics, compare the political thinking of that time with the present."

The teacher may wish to work with a committe of three students to plan the details of the outline the class will follow in writing the paper. Talented students need outlets, and responsibilities such as this will develop their leadership and utilize their abilities constructively.

It would be rather incredible if some kind of discussion did not evolve as a result of these papers. A symposium could be taped and given to the history department for use in its classes or presented as a program for the history or international relations organization in the school.

Instead of writing a paper, each student could prepare a five-minute speech based on the suggested outline and adapted to his book. Each speaker is introduced by a fellow student. The teacher may wish to explain the requisites of an effective speech, and he can find such material in a good public speaking textbook. Thus some specific instruction and practice in a related language arts field can be included, not because it is in the syllabus but, more important, because there is an immediate need and application for it.

If, as they listen to the speeches, students use previously prepared critic sheets for each talk, an additional dimension can be added. The headings would include: "Name of the Speaker," "Subject," and "Name of the Introducer," plus space for a brief critique of the speech. Did it fit the requirements for content? Was delivery effective? The rest of the sheet should be used for notes on the speech proper. At the end of the session, each student collects the sheets criticizing his speech, shares the commentary with his introducer, and glances over the notes taken by his listeners. By the quality of the notes, he can evaluate how effective his speech was, how clearly he made his points, how organized his thinking was, and how attention getting and keeping was his delivery. The teacher may be surprised to discover that this activity involves a form of criticism that requires speakers to think analytically about their effectiveness. Listeners also acquire some practice in another skill — note-taking.

A student timekeeper should warn each speaker when he has a minute left so that all the speeches can be given within a reasonable period. All the books read should be displayed for several days for examination and to encourage voluntary reading by students whose interests have been aroused.

# 35 The Art of Skimming

To train students in a skill some of them lack, i.e., skimming a book rather than reading it thoroughly, choose books that would be classified as relatively easy reading and ask them to skim at least two of them. They then write a letter to anyone in the class either recommending the book or explaining why reading it was a waste of time. In either case, general statements in the 200-word letter must be justified with references and valid arguments for the point of view. Several times a year students should be given this practice in skimming, as it takes repetition to develop the skill. As adults they will often employ it to keep abreast of all the material they will want to read.

# 36 In-Depth Treatment

High school seniors often have only a superficial knowledge of many literary forms because of the haphazard manner of assigning supplementary reading. Drama and biography are two forms especially unfamiliar to most of them. Since most students consider supplementary reading as an isolated assignment requiring the inevitable book report, they will be surprised and eager to cooperate if the teacher announces that, although the daily curriculum will continue to cover all forms of literature, the supplementary reading for the entire semester will concentrate on one form with all book reports cancelled — individual reports, that is. The success of this project will depend to some extent on its initial presentation by the teacher who must point out its benefits to all students, both college-bound and terminal. As with any project, definite goals and limits must be established at the outset.

The second step is to elect a committee of at least six students to cooperate with the teacher in drawing up detailed plans for class approval. The committee decides:

1. The form of literature to be studied — novel, short story, drama, or biography.

2. The reading requirements — no maximum but a minimum of one a month, eight readings a semester, or whatever other scheme they propose and approve. Working rules such as three one-act plays will be the equivalent of one three-act drama must also be clarified.

3. The limitations — students make individual choices, everyone concentrates on the same historical or characteristic classification (For example, if the literary form is drama, they could concentrate on American drama, contemporary theater, or the works of Ibsen, Shaw, Pirandello, Lorca, or O'Neill.), or any other proposal that is practical in terms of the plays available in the school or public library.

The committee chairman reports its suggestions, either announcing a final decision or giving the class an opportunity to vote upon several choices.

Within two weeks each student must submit a list of the authors, titles, and sources of the works he plans to read. Such a listing is mandatory to prevent the reading from becoming desultory. One or two periods of browsing in the library and inspecting book club brochures and paperback catalogs will hasten this preliminary planning. The teacher and his colleagues in the English department may offer to lend suitable volumes from their personal libraries.

The teacher and library staff can also provide each student with a bibliography of books of literary criticism and research to be found in the library and suggest other sources. Some book stores, especially those in college communities, have large selections of literary criticism in paperback form. Each student will be expected to read a minimum number of pages of such criticism, using the indices and tables of contents to find appropriate commentary.

Students work alone throughout the semester except for occasional conferences with the teacher on the progress being made or for individual assistance. His notes on his research reading may be inspected to check on his progress or their effectiveness. The climax of the semester is a paper, perhaps with a 1,500-word limit, based on a combination of the research and the general reading. Everyone can write on the same subject, pick one of several possibilities proposed by the teacher and the student committee, or select his own topic. Broad yet specific subjects such as "The Playwright as a Social Critic," "A Comparative Study of Ibsen, Shaw, and Lorca," "The Nature of Comedy in Drama," "Tragedy, What Is It?" or dozens of variations should enable each student to incorporate the background material into an intelligent analysis of his reading. This work should not be called a term paper or even a research paper because the connotations may suggest copying the ideas of others and parroting them back. All the completed papers can be bound together and placed in the classroom library for use by future students.

A culminating week of oral activities should be considered. There could be 10–15-minute lectures, forums, general discussions, interviews, a reading workshop in which students exchange papers with each other, simple debates, or a bull session involving three or four students who have discovered they have different viewpoints. A teacher knowledgeable in the field of drama or a local or area authority could be invited to lecture in the auditorium to the seniors, with a general invitation extended to all school personnel.

In this sort of personal reading project the stigma of the book report is removed, and every participant feels a rewarding satisfaction in his newly acquired depth of perception. He will incidentally have gained some experience in individual study, which college-bound students are sure to find good preparation for advanced study in any field.

# 37 Let's Debate

The teacher chooses a group of seven who plan their reading around a subject that will provide material for a debate, e.g., the United Nations, foreign aid, American involvement in world affairs, or social needs and problems. The other members of the class can be given a written assignment and will be the audience for the debate. If the teacher is interested in keeping the debate within the English literature field, he can select a topic based on fiction reading, e.g., "Resolved: That contemporary authors will not survive if they continue to employ current styles and techniques." Obviously such topics are more esoteric than the more factual nonfiction debates; but even though high school students will not display adult maturity, they need practice in original thinking.

A conference with the school's debating coach or one of his top debaters will help the group learn how to prepare, but the teacher should spend a period with the entire class discussing the techniques involved in a debate so that at a later date others can participate in one.

The audience determines which side wins the debate and which speaker was the most convincing. Of course it will take part in the question-and-answer period that some forms of debate permit. This activity is excellent therapy for repairing attitudes toward reading and permits students to share an experience with their peers. When the debating coach or several members of the Debating Club act as judges, they will be goaded to better preparation and performance.

# 38 The Historical Approach

It is generally assumed that the more we know about the period during which a book was written, the better we can understand the philosophy of the author, the characters, and all other aspects of the book. Then, too, we can understand our own era better if we have a knowledge of the past. Some upperclassmen under the guidance of a wise teacher may wish to test this theory by studying, for example, 20th-century literature by dividing the period into possible sections:

### 20th-Century American Literature

1. Post-19th-century influences (1900–1910)
   a. 19th-century realism
   b. Industrial Revolution
2. European influence
   a. Freud and others
   b. French novelists
   c. English culture
3. Effects of Wars
   a. World War I
   b. World War II
   c. Korean War
   d. Cold War

4. Current trends and innovations
   (List possibilities up to the present moment)

This activity can be pursued by an individual student whose abilities and interests surpass his classmates' and for whom the teacher must seek more challenging paths of expression or by a small group of six to ten students when their classmates are involved in some simpler reading project. Usually, however, the entire class participates, and the details given here are for this last application; if an individual or small group use this activity, the teacher and the students involved can revise the procedure details.

First everyone in the class selects one novel, one drama, and one biography or nonfiction title from each of the four main periods or subdivisions listed. Due dates are assigned to keep the project moving. Three students capable of or eager to carry out special assignments also read encyclopedias, college texts, or other source books in the library and report back to the class about as much background material on the first literary period as possible. Each uses a lectern to present his lecture and cooperates with his fellow students to avoid repetitious material. The group invites questions from the audience, and if it receives any queries it cannot answer, then it tries to find the answer. The teacher may have to lead this questioning, as high school students may be unfamiliar with the technique of questioning. They can emulate, and will, if the teacher points the way.

The next step is for everyone in the class to read books typical of the second period, again with choices of fiction and nonfiction. This time a different committee of three investigates the background of the period and presents oral accounts to the class. Each student then writes a paper, drawing upon the lectures, on why his book is or is not a good example of the period. The best three papers can be read by their authors or other students who are better readers. Again the use of a simple lectern gives importance and stature to the occasion. Appointing a recording secretary to take notes on the lectures and prepare stencils so that everyone may have copies is a valuable extra.

Another group of three students conducts research on the third period and again each class member selects and reads a book from that era. After the lectures, each student prepares an outline delineating how his reading definitely belongs to or is a maverick of the period. As a teacher knows, some writers are ahead of their time, and some students will be puzzled if their books do not reflect the established and accepted characteristics of a period. Using the outlines only, one row of students at a time sits before the class and is interrogated on why their books were or were not characteristic of the era. They should raise such points as how a writer influenced other writers and what their contributions were. If the teacher wishes to use only one or two rows, the others can submit their written outlines.

If there is a fourth literary period, every student can be instructed to search out data on it and bring his notes to class. Again he selects and reads a book representative of the period. It is desirable for students to vary their choices and read both fiction and nonfiction. Background material can be discussed in one big buzz session in which each class member is expected to contribute while avoiding repetitions.

Obviously this is a long-term activity as the class must, of necessity, consider other aspects of the course curriculum, and it might span a semester or in some classes, two semesters. The teacher is responsible for making sure that adequate background source material is available. He can request the library to place all appropriate books, except encyclopedias and the like, on reserve shelves and can even contribute personal textbooks, which would be protected by a careful check-out system.

Preparing an annotated bibliography of all books read

would be a valuable follow-up. A teacher could also eliminate the secretaries and ask each student to take his own notes on the lectures. This would tie in with a period or two of instruction on the techniques, organization, shortcuts, symbols, appearance, readability, and value of note-taking. Almost all school libraries have books about effective study and work habits, which have chapters on note-taking, and reading these and the suggestions in the students' textbooks could be a specific assignment.

This reading activity and its correlated exercises should expand students' knowledge and give them the satisfaction of sharing their opinions and findings in a practical manner. It offers opportunities for students who crave an outlet for their intellectual curiosity, while less aggressive students have a chance to share responsibility in a less spectacular fashion.

# **39** I Recommend

The English class pretends it is a literary club that once a year donates six books to the city library or to one of its branches. The club meets to consider 12 nominations made by 12 members who volunteered to read books. In three-minute talks they tell the membership about their books and why they feel they are worthy of being among the final six choices. The speakers include such information as the age range of the book's readers, the reasons for the book's value, opinions of authorities, costs, and as many other attention-getting ideas as their young minds can conjure up.

All club members and the teacher have blank sheets on which to record their reactions to each speaker's book. These sheets have columns with these headings: "Title," "Author," "Type of Book," "Effective Points Made by Speaker," "Total Number of Checks," "Speaker's Name." Each time a listening club member thinks a speaker has made a worthwhile point, he records a check in the proper column, and at the conclusion of the meeting he totals his checks and circles the titles of the six books that received the largest number. The ballots are then collected and analyzed and the winners announced. If there is a tie, the presiding officer calls for a show of hands. The teacher thus has the opportunity to introduce some practice in parliamentary procedure, a skill every student needs to fit him for adult responsibilities.

The teacher can assign other groups other activities for reporting on their books. With the novelty faded, repeating this activity with another group would be boring; therefore it is suggested for one group only.


# 40 Bookmarkers for All

This activity is ideal for National Library Week, Catholic Book Week, or Children's Book Week, but need not be confined to such occasions. Sometimes school librarians purchase bookmarks on which the theme of the week and the exhortation to read are printed, but this activity enables everyone in all English classes to participate, although it can be limited to one grade level or one class from each grade level.

No restrictions should be placed on the supplementary reading except that students are to read books for sheer pleasure, joy, or interest. Each student chooses a statement such as those suggested below and writes preferably 25 words and no more than 35 about his book:

> I dare you to read ———.
> Bored? Try reading ———.
> Nothing to do this weekend? Then I suggest you read ———.
> Take my advice; read ———.
> It's new! It's different! It's ———!
> Want to improve your ———? Then read ———.
> I like it. You will too. Read ———.
> Best book of the year! ———.

The teacher and the class can certainly expand this list.

Each student can measure and cut a piece of white or light-colored paper 8 x 2 inches, or for uniformity and convenience a committee can prepare the strips using a paper cutter and appropriate stock. The catchy statement is lettered or typed at the top across the two-inch width, and the 25-word recommendation is written or typed below.

The teacher may ask each student to write two initial recommendations, and during a classroom workshop period a committee can advise on the best choice, pointing out errors in spelling and other technical considerations to be corrected before it is applied to the 8 x 2 inch bookmarker. The use of the student committee gives students of greater ability an opportunity to exercise it; often their peers will accept criticism from them more graciously than from the teacher. Besides, it is certain that this committee will detect the same errors that the teacher has previously noted and this reemphasis from a different critic will drive the correction home.

All the markers can be created at one time, but some can be held for use throughout the year. They may be placed in each book checked out of the library or piled at the check-out desk or on a library display table with the invitation "Have You Read This Book?" prominently printed on an accompanying sign, "Take One!" To achieve wider distribution the markers can be passed out in homerooms or exchanged with other English classes.

# 41 Leading the Horse to Water

When a teacher has a class of students who are reluctant, timid, or suspicious of reading because of lack of success in the past, pressure to read material beyond their abilities and interests, or because they have short attention spans and long reading assignments seem impossibly difficult, he should begin at the level to which they have developed. Rather than forcing artificial tasks upon them, he should try to give them material they will enjoy reading and thus help them to achieve success and gain pleasure from the printed word. The magazine article is an ideal source for this type of reading.

A large and varied stock of magazines can be procured from faculty members, friends, students in other English classes, the librarian, and a visit to a nearby secondhand book and magazine store. Issues of magazines subscribed to by students such as *Scope*, which is published expressly for the reluctant or limited ability reader, should also be collected before initiating this activity. If the group includes students who have technical or psychological problems associated with reading, some juvenile magazines usually intended for younger children can be casually included to meet their needs, but for these students the advice of a reading specialist should be sought and heeded by the classroom teacher.

One day a week is spent reading magazines, and the teacher will be wise to change the assortment each time, adding some issues and removing an equal number.

A procedure such as the following is suggested:

FIRST WEEK: Free reading. The only restriction is that students maintain a quiet atmosphere and be considerate of others. Push six or eight desks together with a supply of magazines scattered on them to prevent walking around. The teacher will not comment on the reading except to help those who ask help in finding articles of interest.

SECOND WEEK: Same reading conditions and same desk arrangement, but set aside five minutes at the end of the period for anyone to recommend a particularly good article he has read. Keep this period short. It is better psychologically to have the bell ring before the suggestions are completed.

THIRD WEEK: Make the groupings smaller for variety, with four desks together and a renewed supply of magazines. The teacher might show the class some of the new magazines to rekindle interest. Allow ten minutes at the end of the period for anyone to tell the class about interesting new ideas or facts he has just read. The teacher may wish to ask for one simple statement from each student, and afterward go back to a student who seemed particularly anxious to expand his original contribution. Someone may even want to ask questions.

FOURTH WEEK: Start the reading session by giving the class an objective such as finding an article on a controversial subject. This will need to be explained with examples keyed to current topics such as civil rights, changes in education, safety devices for new cars, crime control, or urban problems. The teacher who is familiar with his group is the best judge of what subjects it can handle. After the reading, let anyone who wishes to participate contribute to an informal 15-minute discussion.

FIFTH WEEK: Slip into the piles of magazines some more difficult titles to tease students with ability, but continue to supply all types for all interests and reading levels. This week students again use the tables of contents to find articles that appeal to their interests, which may range from makeup for teenagers to the technical aspects of an automobile engine. The teacher circulates to assist those who cannot pinpoint an interest or lack imagination. This time plan for 20 minutes of student discussion and draw in shy, retiring students with subtle questions. One article will probably dominate and catch the interest of the group. If so, the student who read it should be asked to visit the library and bring back at least one book on the subject. He may miss the point that the teacher would like him to read it, and if so, displaying it prominently may have to suffice until the right psychological moment arrives. The teacher might suggest that the student skim through the volume to find more facts that would interest him and class members.

Thus the weeks proceed with the teacher suggesting a book or books that give more details on interests sparked by magazine articles. Unbelievable as it may seem, reluctant readers eventually can conduct good discussion and even debates on articles and related book materials. If oral communication is constantly emphasized, they forget, or perhaps do not realize, that they are reporting on reading. Eventually all students should give lectures or talks.

By the end of the year, some miracles are even possible. Students might produce a class magazine and distribute it to the faculty to show the achievement of which they are capable. They could assume the responsibility of preparing a new column for the school newspaper entitled "With the Current Magazines," which would contain reviews of outstanding articles. Individuals could also write reviews, and a committee select the best ones to submit to the newspaper editor. Bulletin boards that display articles at a comfortable reading level can help maintain interest. The imaginative teacher will find a great ally in the magazine to help reluctant readers.

 **Spell-Down**

After reading a novel, biography, or nonfiction, all class members construct five general questions, each on a 3 x 5 inch card, that could apply to any book in these categories. The student committee editing the questions may ask some individuals to substitute a question that is repetitious of another or to reword a question for clarity. All the cards are placed in a box, the class is divided into two teams, and the old device of a spell-down is brought into play. If a student cannot answer a question on the basis of his book, he is dropped from his team. Success with this activity depends upon framing questions that apply to books in general.

If the entire class is too unwieldy, two teams of five each can compete, with all the class supplying questions as suggested above. Another variation is to weight each question with a point value from 0 to 10, so the two teams try to roll up a score rather than work to eliminate their competitors. The teacher rates the questions for each team's scorekeepers. The winning team might receive some kind of reward such as being excused from an assignment or being presented with a paperback bought with money contributed by the losers. The book can be inscribed with the winners' names and be presented to the class library.

# 43 The Classics Revisited

An encyclopedia is seldom considered a device for stimulating students' reading; however, an examination of the heading "Children's Literature," a division of "Literature" in the *World Book Encyclopedia* will disclose a 15-page listing of important books in this field, which is updated in the annual supplements. The list is divided according to age groupings and will acquaint junior-high youngsters with the basic literature they should read to develop a foundation on which to build their more mature literary appreciation.

All the students investigate possible sources of the titles listed and report their findings to a source committee, which records this information on the bulletin board and also distributes it on dittoed sheets. The class is divided into as many groups as there are copies of the volume of the encyclopedia available. Each student tries to decide what book he will read and gives the title orally to the group chairman, who handles the encyclopedia and reads from it the summary of the selected titles. This is done until all reach definite decisions, but meantime the brief summarizing sentences have acquainted everyone in the group with many books.

After the reading period, the teacher will probably wish to assign to a chosen group the questions contained in this encyclopedia article. Each student can be responsible for preparing orally one answer. The answers to such questions as "What contributions to children's literature did Alfred the Great make?" or "Why did early authors of children's stories not sign their own names?" can be found in this and other encyclopedia volumes. Additional questions can be found in other encyclopedias. After a session spent on these answers, each student can be asked to write one paragraph of 150–200 words using as his topic sentence the encyclopedia description of his book. The sentences copied should be underlined for identification, and the paragraph should elaborate on it by citing examples or illustrations from the book to explain the truth of the sentence(s). As many summaries as possible should be read aloud in class with students exchanging papers. This latter device provides variety and spontaneity often lacking when a student reads his own work; it also necessitates neat handwriting as a courtesy to the reader.

This activity can be adapted for use on the senior high school level for a different purpose with a selected group. Students who intend to become either elementary school teachers or teachers of English on a secondary level form a committee that prepares an oral presentation of the questions and answers suggested by the *World Book Encyclopedia* article on "Children's Literature." They can plan this as a forum discussion or individual speeches. Each student should read three of the books on the junior-high or elementary-age lists and plan a program of reviews, using the descriptions from the encyclopedia as previously suggested. The class pretends to be a parents' child-study group, and the speakers adapt their material to this audience. Since most students anticipate assuming the responsibilities of parenthood at some future time, the project benefits not only the participants who need a background in children's literature but also the listeners who must someday guide their own children's reading.

# 44 Culture Club

In classes of average or superior ability, the stigma of the book report can be eliminated by creating a club such as the

Friday Reading Club, Culture Corner Club, Read for Profit Club, or some other name the students fancy. This club can meet periodically and provide practice in creating a constitution and bylaws and conducting business and a program according to formal parliamentary procedure. An attractive little booklet distributed to the class members can outline the programs for the semester or school year and give the names of chairmen, participants, dates, time, subjects, and books to be discussed at each meeting. This will enhance the project and give it a realistic adult tone in imitation of the clubs to which some parents belong. The creation of this program or yearbook as it is sometimes called can provide an outlet for students who need unusual activities to maintain their interest in school routine. Many of the activities described in this book could serve as program possibilities for club meetings.

 **How To**

We live in a how-to era with books, magazine articles, lectures, home-study courses, gadgets, and tools purporting to teach or help us how to do many things by ourselves. Most students do not read enough nonfiction, and this activity is a stimulant to change that situation. Since the oral feature is very time-consuming, the teacher may wish to assign it to only a portion of his class and give the rest a different project.

The theme governing the reading choice is "How to ————," but students must realize that appropriate books need not contain these two words in their titles. For example, *I Wanted to Be an Actress* by Katharine Cornell could be "how to become a successful actress," *Inside Africa* by John

Gunther is "how to understand the emerging nations," *The Book of Play Production* by Milton Smith is "how to direct a play," and *The Joy of Music* by Leonard Bernstein is "how to enjoy music." Of course there are scores of books in the school library having "how to" in the title: *How to Get a Job in Television, How to Play Tennis,* and *How to Study and Prepare for Exams,* for example.

Each student involved prepares an eight to ten-minute how-to speech based on his reading. He must use visual aids such as the blackboard, charts, graphs, pictures, or three-dimensional objects appropriate to his subject. He may employ an opaque or overhead projector or part of a filmstrip. Using notes only (no written manuscript is required) he practices to contain his speech within the time limits and to bring profitable pleasure to his audience of do-it-yourselfers.

# 46 With Illustrations

Each senior high school student chooses a nonfiction book that deals directly with his major field of interest — art, music, science, language, history, or vocational education. After reading for the enjoyment and value the volume has for him, he writes a critique illustrated with reproductions of charts, graphs, or drawings contained in the book or pictures created by himself. If the student is majoring in English, for example, he might choose to read a book on the history of the theater and one of the illustrations could be a copy of a drawing of a Greek theater he found in an encyclopedia or other reference book. The illustrations should be well arranged and closely related in location to the written material they clarify, enhance, or explain. The five best critiques can be read to the class, and all of them should make an attractive, eye-catching exhibit.

Instead of writing a paper, oral visual presentations can be prepared instead. The teacher divides the class into small groups according to their major interests, and each group plans a discussion and selects appropriate illustrative material. Every participant will be expected to introduce his book and utilize its content to elaborate on the subject the group is exploring.

# **47** Poetry Anthologies

An effective way to teach poetry to general classes is to employ the theme or subject approach. To stimulate individual reading of poetry, compiling original anthologies that reflect the individual interests of students can be successful because the limitations and restrictions are few.

Each boy and girl chooses one theme from a list suggested by the students themselves — loneliness, religion, brotherhood, humor, courage, travel, farm and country, despair, contemporary problems, music, civil rights, personal freedom, or many others. From poetry anthologies, magazines containing poetry, or general anthologies containing some poetry, students find, by browsing or through the indices or tables of contents, poems appropriate to their chosen themes. Each student works alone fulfilling the requirements listed for his grade level on the accompanying chart. His anthology will be his own individual creation.

Writing original poems is suggested for upper grades if the teacher wishes to include this assignment. He also decides whether to give any instruction on meter, rhyme, or other

## Original Poetry Anthology Requirements

| Grade Level | Cover | Preface | Introductory Composition | Long Poem Excerpts | Minimum Number of Poems | Illustrations | Original Poem on Theme |
|---|---|---|---|---|---|---|---|
| 7 | Original or traced illustrations or pictures | Why I chose this theme; 100 words | None | None | 5 | Optional | Optional |
| 8 | As above | 100 words | The origins of poetry; 75-100 words | None | 7 | Optional | Optional |
| 9 | As above | 125 words | The poem I liked best and why; 150 words | None | 10 | Optional | Required minimum of 4 lines |
| 10 | As above | 125 words | How the poet creates pictures; 200 words | 1 | 10 | Optional | Required minimum of 6 lines |
| 11 | As above | 150 words | Why do poets write poetry? 250-300 words | 2 | 12 | Optional | Required minimum of 8 lines |
| 12 | As above | 150 words | What devices do poets use? Explain; 300-350 words | 3 | 12 | Optional | Required minimum of 8 lines |

poetic devices prior to this creative work or to omit formal instruction and allow the student poets to write naturally. Of course, the best original poems should be shared and the poets given recognition.

Expanding on these initial steps, an anthology project can include a more detailed study of poetry. The best compositions from the anthologies can be projected so the entire class can see the elements of effective writing and the development of ideas and feelings. In the twelfth grade, a discussion led by a student can be conducted. In all classes each student can be expected to explain his theme and read one poem as an example of his choice. The best original poems should be submitted to the school newspaper or magazine or to student magazines or contests.

If the area boasts of a poet, he could be invited to read his own poetry and perhaps some of his favorite poets. Playing records of poets or professional readers is a fitting climax to a poetry unit. Perhaps three talented readers could present a formal poetry reading using stools and stands in imitation of the current programs by professional actors. They can make their selections from the students' anthologies, including some of the original poems. A coffee-house style poetry reading, complete with guitar accompaniment, might find favor with the class.

# 48 Interludes with Poetry

A teacher is advised to introduce this activity by referring to the popularity of some poetry among young people and the many poetry readings taking place in the cities and on the campuses. Students spend two or three periods browsing and reading poems from magazines and books in the classroom or in the library. They compile a list of all the poems they have read to completion and on the last day must be prepared to read two poems that particularly appealed to them. No detailed analyses nor reasons why they appealed are expected. However, after the teacher has examined the lists of poems, he leads a discussion the following day and by questioning individual students and perhaps asking them to read parts of the poems, he can skillfully project the reason poetry has a special appeal — it is the literature of the individual! Some records of poets reading their own works or actors reading a variety of poetry could be played, or talented teachers or students could tape their own readings of poems.

# **49** Poetry Through the Years

Pre-college students of high ability can benefit from an in-depth poetry study. Acquaintance with poetic terminology is the initial requirement. Source books that list and discuss poetic terms can be assembled either in the classroom or the library for workshop sessions during which each student seeks out as many definitions as time allows. He must be able, using his notes, to explain the words, whether simple ones like "elegy," technical ones like "Elizabethan sonnet," or elusive ones like "free verse." During one or two classroom sessions students share their findings, taking notes during the discussion directed by the teacher. If desired, a master sheet of the most important terms can be prepared by a student committee.

An historical format for further poetry study is recommended. Depending upon the size of the class, each student is assigned to a committee to research one period, such as religious poetry of the colonists, the national era, the Civil War period, or World War II to the present. Although the assignment sounds formidable, extensive resources are not required as the recognized encyclopedias have excellent summaries of literary periods. Each group chooses a spokesman who reports orally the pooled findings of committee members. These talks should emphasize the effects historical events had upon poetry, the chief poets of the period, the famous poems of the era, and the general characteristics of the poetry. If representative poems are read to illuminate general statements, understanding will be greater. If possible, the chairman makes the notes for his speech on a ditto sheet he distributes to class members to help them take organized notes for future use.

Several sessions follow during which each group presents readings of reasonable length, no less than five. Listeners should scan the dittoed sheet and their notes to be alert to the significance of the poems in their eras. Perhaps student ingenuity can dream up unusual settings for these poetry reading sessions. An alternate idea is to have each student work alone, contributing facts and poems during sessions guided by the teacher.

Some ideas to consider during the discussion periods are: Why do we like this poet and his work? Why not? Which poet of the period did the group find to have the greatest appeal? Is this poem out of fashion today? Why was it popular? Is it difficult to read or understand? Why? Did religious beliefs or political or social situations affect the poem? The teacher can help the student chairmen create additional questions.

At the conclusion of the unit, all the chairmen make a summation of conclusions about the period of literature and how it is part of the complete study that has been conducted. Bulletin board displays in the room should have kept pace with the in-depth study as it progressed.

Creative students may contribute poems written in imitation of the style or technique of some of the poets studied, and they can be read during an informal recital session. In fact, a contest with prizes is incentive to spark this creativity. A field trip to a local college to examine the original manuscript and rare book departments of the library may provide an opportunity to see manuscripts that show a poet's repeated efforts to rework (his) creation to achieve perfection of ideas and diction.

# 50 Negatively Speaking

Students may respond to a negative approach to the book report. Ask them to write a paper after completing a reading assignment on "Why ———— should not read this book." If given free reign to use their imaginations as they wish in filling the blank, they will little suspect that this novel negative approach is compelling them to think positively.

Reluctant readers sometimes have negative personalities or attitudes, and a day of negative book reports on the theme "I Didn't Like This Book" might be effective. When their classmates challenge false or incomplete ideas, students will discover that few books are universally disliked. They will also discover that, in most cases, the reading was not completely useless. Lively oral sessions can develop from these negative approaches, bringing about some positive thinking and conclusions and giving students an opportunity to gripe under constructive circumstances. Adults know that to have to concur without occasional disagreement is not only boring but impossibly unrealistic. Why then expect young people not to be equally bored by acquiescence?

# 51 Fun with Book Jackets

A large collection of book jackets are examined and discussed to analyze the techniques of copywriting. Some may be projected on a screen for the entire class to evaluate, and their characteristics, such as well-chosen, colorful vocabulary, economy of words, and appeal to the curiosity and emotions of readers, can be listed on the blackboard. Students will probably agree that the objective of the jacket is to orient a prospective reader to enough information about the locale, characters, and plot to make him want to read the book.

After class members have read a variety of types of books that have jackets, they study the first sentence of the advertising copy for meaning, scope, and implications and then use it as the topic sentence in a paragraph of elaboration. For example, "———— is the story of the origins of the Cold War" might be the first sentence; the student analyzes why this statement is apropos to the basic content of the reading. He copies in like fashion each sentence from the jacket copy, following each with a paragraph expounding his reactions, either positive or negative. The length of the paragraphs will depend upon the ability of the individual to handle words and original ideas. If the jacket copy is lengthy, the student can select the five sentences most significant to him.

A reversal of this technique may be more successful with superior ability students who enjoy challenging assignments. They read books that have no jackets and write their own original copy. If composition skills are to be emphasized, instruct them to divide their paper vertically with a three-inch margin on the left side. On the right side they write a complimentary book review. They re-examine their reviews and, using scrap paper, determine how to compress long, involved sentences into phrases or single words woven into short effective sentences. For example, "This book would appeal to many types of readers" could become "has universal appeal." Practice in economy of style and precision in vocabulary enriches the intellectual analysis of the reading. Areas in the right-hand column are bracketed, and opposite them, in the left margin, a condensation is written. The writing in this left column should be a smooth-flowing paragraph condensing the rambling material on the right. Of course, no professional copywriter works in this way. He concentrates from the outset on statements that will intrigue, interest, and persuade a reader to buy or read the book. Some students who have studied composition techniques and been coached in the basic elements of selling could try writing direct and original jacket copy.

Average ability students who have read books without jackets can create original jackets complete with pictures, line drawings, type design, and, most important, a blurb about the book and a sketch of the author. Posting these jackets on a bulletin board can stimulate additional reading among the viewers.

# **52** Novels Under the Microscope

After reading several novels, students are given copies of the three paragraphs below and instructed to write an analysis of how the assertions in one of the paragraphs applies to their reading, using all the books for reference. If only one novel has been read for this assignment, they should be encouraged to refer to novels read in the past as well as the current reading.

1. Contrary to the frequently expressed idea, novels do not hold a mirror up to life. Real life seems to have no plot that moves from level to level with clearly traceable motivations and one big climax that can be labeled the turning point. There are other differences between life and fiction that refute the statement that novels are lifelike. Referring to the novel(s) read, attempt to prove the unreality of most novels. Support the ideas promoted.

2. A strong and memorable character emerges because of struggle, and his struggle never stops. First define the terms as they are understood and then set forth by example, explanation, or argumentation specific instances of the truth of the first sentence.

3. Sometimes a novelist shifts his point of view during the course of the action. Is this true of the novel just read? Determine the author's point of view and how it affected the theme, setting, characters, and even dialogue, philosophy, and style.

As a variation of the foregoing, choose, either by ballot or appointment, six-eight students to make notes on one of the three paragraphs and let them present a discussion before their classmates who are writing papers and who can propose questions for the group after the general commentary has been completed.

A further variation would be to follow the first plan and then have students exchange papers and rate them from ten for excellent down to one for inadequate. This rating may be placed on a prepared sheet that has space for the names of the student writer and the student critic, plus space for giving the reason for the rating with suggestions, if possible, for improvement. When the rating blanks are returned to the students near the end of the period, the teacher might lead a discussion of the major faults in their expository writing.

# 53  Hollywood

Hollywood and the entertainment world use superlatives to advertise their products, and a clever yet constructive method of developing reactions to books utilizes the same technique. From the following list of suggested words each student chooses an assigned number of words to use as keys to his reactions to his reading. The required number of superlatives might vary from five for grade-seven students to ten for grade-twelve critics. The chosen superlatives are lettered or typed in capital letters and are followed by quite specific explanations in a series of coordinated sentences. An unexplained application such as "FASCINATING style" is not satisfactory. Satisfactory explanations would be:

FASCINATING method of plot development. Each chapter moves back and forth in locale and characters. Alternate chapters are two separate plots, which eventually are woven together cleverly to bring out the theme of the novel that evil brings its own reward and to each evildoer in a different manner, sometimes physically and sometimes mentally or psychologically."

CANDID treatment of his chief character, ————. He is not a likeable man whom a person would choose to pattern his life after, because he is greedy, immoral, and cruel even to those he loves, his wife and daughter. His campaign to plot the financial destruction of a business associate is the pivot, however, on which his own destruction revolves eventually.

PROVOCATIVE theme is the chief characteristic of ————. Not many authors probe so deeply into some of the corruption beneath the surface of American institutions that too often are considered beyond criticism. He spares no one involved in the crooked politics of the day, and the pictures he creates of the ward bosses of the metropolitan areas are scathing!

The students may use these words as well as additional ones contributed by them and their teacher:

| | | |
|---|---|---|
| First-rate | Dramatic | Engrossing |
| Superb | Genuine | Impeccable |
| Enlightening | Generous | Enduring |
| Astonishing | Colossal | Lasting |
| Amazing | Conspicuous | Enthusiastic |
| Invaluable | Effervescent | Realistic |
| Honest | Inspirational | Admirable |
| Entertaining | Compulsive | Ambitious |
| Authentic | Captivating | Forceful |
| Distinguished | Illuminating | Durable |
| Exciting | Intriguing | Incredible |
| Singular | Compassionate | Remarkable |
| Revolutionary | Memorable | Notable |
| Important | Commendable | Praiseworthy |

# 54 Looking at the Experts' Work

A small group of four-six students can collect an equal number of book reviews from newspapers and magazines. The reviews must have quality and cover a variety of fiction and nonfiction fields. Each member prepares an oral analysis, recording his observations on 3 x 5 inch cards. While he speaks, the review is projected for the class and, if necessary, he can use the blackboard to list his points.

In conferring with the committee, the teacher may wish to suggest the use of these yardsticks: Does the reviewer skim the surface or does he probe with perception? Does he dodge issues or meet them squarely? Show proof of answer. What is the skeletal outline of the review the writer followed? Write this outline on the board so it can be copied in the students' notebooks during the talk.

The student speakers underline in the reviews all unusual expressions, words, or phrases that contribute to making meanings clear. In a contrasting color (red, for example) they underline all the transitional words and phrases that blend the ideas, maintain the continuity, and progress the logic of the thoughts. They include a discussion of the conclusions the reviewers reached and indicate the point at which this occurred. Unity in the structure of tying the opening and closing ideas is examined, and the weak aspects of the review are mentioned, if they exist, as well as the outstanding attributes of the writer. They may speculate on the effect of the review on the books' sales or popularity. The audience may be invited to comment at suitable times.

All students now choose one of the six outlines they have had explained to them in oral and in written form and use it to write a review of a book they have read. When necessary, adaptations may be made. The reviews are collected, and each of the original speakers is given all those criticisms that followed his outline. He reads and evaluates the writing for organization, content, use of transitionary words and phrases, and general vocabulary as well as the mechanics of spelling, punctuation, and grammar. Each committee member chooses the one review that best satisfied the assignment, and these reviews are shared with the entire class. At the conclusion of this project, students will have been introduced to four to six books besides their own reading choice and to a wealth of practical experience in writing and composition techniques.

# 55 Drama Critics

After class members have read three- or five-act plays, they are told that they are to imagine themselves members of the staff of a theatrical publication. The teacher will want to have some examples for students to examine and read during a class period to help them set standards for the writing expected and to acquaint them with the style of the magazines and the types of articles published. Back numbers of such magazines are available in stores specializing in secondhand books and periodicals.

Each student is to write either a review or a magazine article based on his play, pretending that his editor has given him the assignment. He may imagine that his review is the result of a performance he has seen or he may review it from a literary point of view only. The magazine article can deal with controversial or literary aspects of a play.

Here is a list of thought-provokers to help students analyze their reading. They will assist them to discover in the play and in their own minds the ideas they wish to communicate:

1. Who or what is the protagonist? The antagonist? What is the conflict between them?
2. Climax emerges from a series of crises. Explain the sequence of crises as well as the details of the climax and its ultimate significance and effect.
3. Did the trend of the plot make the end inevitable? Explain.
4. Is the conclusion satisfactory? Logical? Disturbing? Justified? Significant? Philosophical? Final? Destructive? Substantiate the reason for the choice.
5. What examples of good playwriting can be cited?
6. Which is more important, plot or character? Explain.

7. Examine the truth of the statement that every scene in a play must have dramatic purpose and that this must be achieved with economy. Prove using four scenes.
8. Was there falling action after the climax? What was its purpose? What effect did the playwright achieve if the ending itself was the climax?
9. Which key character helped to shape the sequence and outcome of the plot? Did any other character assist? How did the playwright build the character for this purpose?
10. Was any character a victim in any sense? Explain.
11. Was the play an insight into human values? In what way?

The foregoing should not be considered an outline for the review or article but merely a guideline to help students think through an analysis of their plays. However, the teacher may wish to change the assignment to a critical review of the play using one, several, or all of these considerations, arranged in any order the student critic desires. Perhaps the best article or review might find its way into the school newspaper or literary magazine as a special feature written by a "guest" contributor.

# **56** Abridged Editions

For many reasons involving personality and daily obligations many reluctant, but not necessarily incapable, readers find long reading assignments unpleasant or impossible. A book club of long standing, The Reader's Digest Condensed Book Club, caters to the needs of these people plus good readers whose busy lives permit limited time for reading. Friends and faculty who have volumes they have read are usually willing to lend or give books for students who do not have copies. They need not be the latest issues as titles are chosen to be of lasting interest. The teacher will find condensed versions of contemporary books allies in working with reluctant readers who do and can read but not often. This activity can also be used with competent readers as the written assignment is excellent for developing ability in comparative thinking.

The teacher may wish to lecture on the advantages and disadvantages of the condensed book and the skill required of the condensers, and he will want to treat honestly the problem of class members who are bored with or adverse to reading thick volumes of fiction or nonfiction.

After each student has read a complete volume or a mixture from several volumes, he is instructed to write a summary of his reaction. Some guidelines such as the following may be suggested:

1. If two of the selections were novels, compare them as to style of writing, author's intent, theme, impact, importance, and degree of popularity they are likely to enjoy.
2. Choose the one selection that made the greatest impression on you either because of its uniqueness, readability, universality of theme, subject matter, character portrayal, or other reason and explain its impact on you.
3. Some writers are more concerned with the spiritual than the material well-being of their characters. Their attacks are directed not primarily against political, economic, or social wrongs but against the prevailing climate of men's minds and attitudes that lead to abuses. They endeavor to stir the reader to realize that "man does not live by bread alone." How does this theory apply to at least one book in this volume?
4. The art of titling books is significant and purposeful. Choose three selections and explain the meaning, importance, source, or contribution of the title.
5. Choose three protagonists from three different books and

state the main confrontation each encountered. Did he face it successfully? Explain.

6. Choose one author who used the technique of employing a minor character to reveal the main character. Explain how he did this.

7. Imagine you are one of the original board of judges who choose these particular selections. Write a brief 25-35-word statement about each selection recommending that it be included in a book selection. If you read a book you did not like, feel free to give your adverse criticism, even though, obviously, you have been overruled by the other judges and the editor.

All these approaches cannot, of course, be used simultaneously. None of the requirements are long because reluctant readers object to lengthy written assignments as vociferously as extended reading assignments.

# 57 Literary Criticism

After an eleventh- or twelfth-grade class has read fiction or nonfiction, their teacher can introduce them to the literary criticism found in quality magazines and books. Reading examples will help establish the goals of developing style and content that the assignment infers. Although the book read will be the basis for their criticism, other books may be included for purposes of comparison.

The following statements are possible subjects for essays of literary criticism:

1. Authors are men behind masks.
2. Protest is the battle cry of social reform.

3. (Title of book) has a strong but complicated thesis that affects the plot, characterizations, and even the style.

4. Some fiction writers are sociologists.

5. Some writers do not attack a problem directly but rather the cause that created it. Sometimes they promote a solution; occasionally they state a premise, expecting it to serve as a catalyst for action by experts who have the means of solution. This author is such a writer.

6. All fiction writers are philosophers.

7. If we consider the definition of an essayist as one who attempts to do something in written form by weighing, balancing, describing, or analyzing a situation, then the novelist is an essayist. This book is a fine example of this theory.

8. This book is an accurate reflection of the emotional, psychological, and sociological temper and mood of the times.

9. Never underestimate the power of the novelist.

10. The liberation of the writer today.

11. The potency of words.

12. Fact in fiction.

13. The changing face of biography.

14. New worlds of understanding through books.

15. The biographer: a maker of heels or heroes.

16. Show me what the age is reading, and I can tell you the nature of the times.

17. Best sellers prove nothing.

18. Man in fiction is not man in life.

19. Where goes today's theater?

20. Drama is the portrayal of man at his best and at his worst.

The outstanding essay can be studied for its positive qualities: Why was it logical? What conclusions did it propose? What techniques made it effective? The poorest essay could be duplicated with double spacing and wide margins and distributed for students to correct spelling, punctuation, and structural errors and to improve the vocabulary. The critics can use the interlinear space as well as the margins to comment on the organization or lack of it, paragraph development, and general unity. They can include a final statement on the reasons for its weakness, mentioning the development of ideas, arguments, or premises. The student who needs this help will benefit from such criticism, and the others will reap the advantages that always come from analytical thinking.

# 58 Words! Words! Words!

Every writer should periodically rejuvenate his vocabulary discarding hackneyed words and expressions for refreshing new words that will give depth and meaning to his written and oral expression. The book report as executed by many students is especially vulnerable to repetitious terminology. In desperation one teacher outlawed the word "interesting" and even that minor change worked miracles in the substitutes students were forced to employ. The teacher who is conducting a regular vocabulary development program as an integral phase of the English course can use lists suggested in the state syllabus, suggested lists in the appendix of the students' textbooks, and a daily consideration of words encountered in literature study units. An additional ally in practical vocabulary enrichment can be the book report, written or oral. It is well known that the avid reader, student or adult, boasts an extensive vocabulary, for reading is the surest means of gaining acquaintance with words. Teachers must face the fact that all their students are not voracious readers and therefore they must resort to artificial, contrived methods that can never be completely successful.

The teacher can instigate this activity with a class period of discussion and illustration stressing the poverty of students' vocabulary in one or two sets of book report papers. Projecting some of these examples varies the lecture or oral presentation and helps students recognize the need for self-improvement in expression.

The class is divided into many small committees not exceeding three members to engage in a month-long word discovery project. The words to be sought are to be particularly applicable to analysis of characters, setting, authors' style, plot, and other usual elements involved in book reviews. Weekly sessions are scheduled for oral presentations by the chairman of each group to clarify meanings and potential uses and weed out useless contributions that are obscure. Either dittoed lists prepared by a secretary or notes taken by the students will build up a list of vocabulary possibilities.

Each committee might be assigned specific sources as possibilities for exploration and discovery such as:

1. The sports pages of at least four issues of two different newspapers.
2. Editorials from newspapers and magazines.
3. Articles from three or four literary magazines.
4. Front pages from many issues of a variety of newspapers.
5. A complete Sunday edition of a metropolitan newspaper with each section assigned to a committee, e.g., drama and entertainment, sports, news-of-the-week, business, general news, society news, magazine and book review supplements, with one committee analyzing the advertisements for sparking new words.
6. Book jackets.
7. Four or five nonfiction books of current interest.
8. A representative selection of biographies.
9. Books of literary criticism.
10. Contributions from a book of synonyms to substitute for some of the old favorites such as "interesting" and the other worn-out words on which too many students hang their tired ideas.

In the weekly analytical sessions the teacher clarifies meanings and with the students works out possible applications for the most valuable contributions although the final uses will depend upon the students' imagination and ability. The final phase of the month-long study will be to write a book review containing at least ten of the new words or phrases. They are underlined for easy identification. At first both the teacher and the students may find this method somewhat artificial, but as the list is employed again and again with all the written and oral reports required during the course, the students will find it a stimulus to their thinking in book reviewing.

Just as this activity began with a negative appraisal of poor vocabulary usage, it should conclude positively with sessions pointing up improvements in the students' writing as well as additional weaknesses or problems still unresolved by some students.

# 59 Let's Listen

Because the time involved would make it impossible for everyone in a class to participate in this activity, just three students are chosen or elected to prepare a full period of lectures on their recent reading. Each talk is to be illustrated, not with pictures but with taped excerpts from the books. The speaker selects excerpts appropriate to his needs and intentions and supervises the taping of dialogue, narration, or a combination of both. Family members, schoolmates, or other adults are the readers, not the student himself. If the voices of talented young people suggested by the dramatics coach are used, greater audience attention may be maintained. Several short excerpts are more effective than one long one.

The student lecturer prepares a 12-15-minute speech that includes at least two excerpts to illustrate his points. They may demonstrate style, reveal the theme, show characterization, disclose attitudes or prejudices, or depict some other feature. For example, if a speaker is discussing a Hemingway novel and wishes to demonstrate the laconic style so characteristic of him, a typical example would be enlightening.

The teacher should advise the speakers to practice their talks, either operating the recorder themselves or relying on an assistant. The best speech could be offered as a program for a library or literary club meeting in the school.

# **60** The Visual Treatment

During one class period three selected students can present oral book reviews that are enhanced and enlivened with colored slides or transparencies, commercial or personal. The rest of the class will fulfill their book review obligations in another format, probably a written one. The teacher will want to emphasize the importance of thoroughly investigating the availability of suitable slides before the students become too involved in preparing their speeches. Slides may be available from the office or supply rooms of each department in the school, the school library, or the audio-visual department maintained separately in some schools. The possibility of borrowing slides from family, friends, or faculty members should not be overlooked. An SOS on the faculty bulletin board might be productive.

The teacher should caution the students that this is not to be a slide viewing with incidental talk but rather the reverse, with a limited number of transparencies shown for the specific purpose of illuminating, elaborating on, or explaining the substance of the book talk. For example, if one of Dickens' novels is the subject, slides depicting Dickens' London and its environs, which were the scenes of so many of his novels, can be introduced to increase audience attention and the speaker's success. If an American novel with a midwestern background is being reviewed, photographs of that area today are just as representative of the topography and atmosphere as in the covered-wagon days, especially pictures of areas unspoiled by civilization. Travel books are obviously good choices for this treatment, but close teacher supervision will be necessary to prevent such a speech from becoming a series of slide showings strung together with incidental commentary. The speech is of prime importance; the slides are incidental. There may be occasions, however, when the teacher purposely invites a student from another class to give a profusely illustrated lecture to rouse the interest of reluctant readers in reading travel or adventure books.

# **61** Rebels, One and All

This biography activity is recommended for a class with a preponderance of young rebels who are not juvenile delinquents but a lively group who usually disagree with the *status quo* and are full of youthful energy that would change everybody and everything. The danger with such a group is that unless the teacher channels the rebelliousness into a constructive activity, it will remain negative and undirected. On some appropriate day he can discuss at length the part rebels have played in changing the history of the world, inviting contributions and comments from the class. Of course, his thesis will be that these rebels were men and women who were dissatisfied with things as they found them but they stopped complaining and did something about the situations. Each student is then given the assignment of returning to class on a later date with the names of at least three rebels in this category.

Where do they find such names? They can ask teachers in the history, English, or science departments for suggestions or examine sources in the library. They can discuss the matter with their parents or search their own minds for a remembrance of previous knowledge about such persons. A list can be typed up for the use of all class members, who are directed to find biographies about some of these men and women who spent lifetimes finding better answers and better ways, and left a better world for all who followed after them.

Oral presentations by the students are a logical outgrowth of this reading experience. Some may wish to give individual talks; others may join a small group to work as a unit; or class members who have diverse views may present a debate. Hopefully, the conclusion will be that rebels are necessary, not rebels who think and act negatively for the destruction of everything they oppose but rebels who think and act positively to move their world forward.

Less able groups who are not usually interested in intellectual subjects and may themselves be guilty of much misdirected rebellion will enjoy these presentations and will respond well as the subject is within their scope. They may or may not recognize that they have been tricked into doing some worthwhile reading, plus indulging in constructive thinking and maybe some readjustments in their personal ideologies. What better objective could a reading activity have!

A real coup would be to have a young musician in the

group compose a ballad in typical folk song style about one or several of the rebels and, accompanied by a guitarist, sing it. If there is no musical talent in the class, maybe there is a balladeer who can write a poem and recite it accompanied by background music provided by a record. The teacher may have to play some records of this type of poem or song for students to imitate. When reading leads to active communication and into creativity, it has achieved its highest goal.

# 62 Ads and More Ads

After reading fiction or nonfiction books each student chooses one of the following types of advertisement to produce:

1. He writes a plan for a TV commercial about his book. This should include all necessary dialogue as well as a description of the action and pictures that accompany it.
2. He plans and prepares a dummy for a magazine or newspaper advertisement, pretending that the book is newly published and being introduced to the reading public. This ad need not be a work of art but a work or planning sheet; therefore it can be a sheet of paper the size of the ad with the lettering, copy, illustrations, or decorations pasted on in bits and pieces.
3. He can design a 2 x 4 foot poster to be used in a bookstore to advertise his book. Again, the poster does not have to be a finished product, but it should contain all the material that is to be printed and include a rough sketch of the layout with

possible illustrations indicated by pasting on pictures or designs found in other sources.

4. He can design a bulletin board for the school library, hall, or English class. After determining the actual size of the available space, he plans on paper the details of his display, which will include written and pictorial materials. He may wish to emphasize his book among other related titles if the space is too large to promote a single book. He need not execute the actual bulletin board, but the written materials should be fully developed and the illustrations described or sketched.

5. He can design a case exhibit for the library or hall, whichever is actually in the school. The emphasis must be on his book, but he can expand the theme to include related books and materials, including pamphlets available in the library if the subject area of his reading was nonfiction.

The teacher will find that this activity has many possibilities and much flexibility. He can decide to give the assignment as described here, to give only one of the five choices to everyone, or to assign one choice to each row or group within the class. He should also decide on some kind of judging whereby a student or faculty committee chooses and awards gold, red, and blue ribbons to the promotion ideas considered the most original and worthwhile.

# 63 The Biographer's Art

Biography is difficult to review with any single standard outline or plan because biographers develop their material in a variety of ways. Some use a chronological framework, others a thematic format, and still others a loose memoir or series of letters or diary entries. Also some students read biography easily and naturally, while others find it difficult. For this reason, several suggestions are given here so that the teacher can select the scheme most suitable for his students.

After the class has read biographies, a period can be devoted to an adaptation of the old game of 20 questions. As many numbers as there are students in the class are marked on separate slips of paper and mixed thoroughly in a box or bag. Each student picks a number. Number one stands before the group. He does not reveal the name of his book or its subject. Class members may ask him 20 questions in an effort to determine the identity of his biographee. The important difference between this activity and the original game is that in the latter the questions are framed to required yes or no responses, whereas in this game the questions are framed to elicit full sentence replies. For example, instead of "Were you born in the United States?" the correct form would be "Where were you born?" The object, of course, is for a student to survive as many questions as possible before someone guesses the name of his biographee. The game proceeds with each student taking his turn in order. If the teacher wishes to limit the game to one period, students who did not have an opportunity to participate can be given a bonus of no report of any kind—this reading was for fun only!

A second method of reviewing biographies employs essay questions to help students write studies of the biographies they have read.

A suitable title must accompany each study; typical examples are: "A Man for All Times," "She Shaped History," "Rebel in Uniform," "She Shook the Family Tree," "History Made Him Great," "He Took a Chance," "A Ripple on the Sands of Time," "His Success Was Inevitable," or "A Likable Failure."

The teacher may duplicate the following questions and distribute them to the class so that they all can be used simultaneously. Each student can adapt the set of questions he selects to fit his reading, thus assuring variety to the approaches students take to their writing and the discussion that may follow.

1. Describe the opening of the biography. Where or how does it end? What are the subject's basic drives and compulsions? How did they and his family background influence him? What were his weaknesses? Was he aware of them? How did he cope with them? What was the primary difficulty he had to overcome at any time in his life? What was his idea of success? Did he achieve it? Analyze the writing style of the book. Was it effective for presenting this biography?
2. Discuss briefly the reasons for the popularity of biography today. Does the author have status in the literary world? Should he? What period of the subject's life was covered by the book? Was this a significant choice? What was the purpose of the writing? If you were to write a biography on this person, would you choose the same span of time? Explain. Was his career a conflict in any way for him? Does the man or the book have weaknesses? In conclusion, write three meaty sentences that fully summarize the subject of the biography in the manner that the author presented him.
3. Begin with a sentence quote from the book that is significant or fundamental to the biographee. Briefly sketch an anecdote that is a key to his personality. Was his education a significant factor in his life? Did he have intuitive gifts such as sympathy, understanding, intelligence, or patience? How did they influence his accomplishments? What was the biographer's technique — anecdotal, critical, or philosophical? If he is critical, show how. Does he set himself up as the voice of authority? Prove the points made. What conclusions are reached?
4. What part of the subject's life is covered, including the

importance of the period? Did the biographer have any association with the subject? Is this fact significant? What are the subject's greatest contributions? Did he ever suffer in any way? Explain. Is the book an honest appraisal? Explain.

5. Compose a summarizing sentence about the subject of the biography based on the author's presentation. Using that summary as a topic sentence, write a biographical essay that would be worthy of inclusion in a collection of short biographies in an imaginary book titled *"Men and Women Young People Should Know."*

# **64** Let's Write a Book

After students have read nonfiction books that covered a wide range of subjects, they are told that they are now going to write a manuscript suitable for submission to a publisher of paperbacks. The title of the book might be "Great Works of Nonfiction," "Significant Nonfiction of the Past 25 Years," or "Nonfiction for Every Teenager." Each student is to write a chapter that will be a review of his book. The title should indicate his approach, with the title of the book as a subtitle. Titles might be: The Past Is Never Dead, Off to Far Places, Bringing the Near East Nearer, The Right to Defend the Right, or Campaigning for a Lost Cause.

The authors should elect an editor and an assistant to supervise the correction of the individual chapters. Another group can supervise the typing of the entire manuscript and the preparation of the title page, table of contents, preface, and a suitable binding. Although this is only a dry run of the process a book manuscript undergoes in reality, it does afford students an opportunity to aim for high standards. The finished manuscript should be placed in the school library or in a special section of the classroom library reserved for this purpose. Seeing one's name in print can inspire greater effort and interest. One student should be delegated to write an article for the school newspaper telling of the class project of creating a book, giving the names of the editor and his staff as well as the contributors and mentioning the fact that it is permanently in the aforementioned section of the library.

# **65** Those Transitionary Phrases

Logical thinking is required for good expository writing, and the book review assignment can provide practice in developing this ability. Transitional words and phrases are devices that can aid a writer to connect his sentences, paragraphs, and the flow of his thoughts in logical progression. They also add fluidity to his style. The class studies textbook materials on transitionary words and phrases and examines magazine articles, editorials, essays, and book reviews for effective examples of the technique. Instructing students to underline all the transitionary devices in a magazine article and to analyze the effect of each enables the teacher to check their understanding of the basic principles and rules.

Each student writes a book report using an essay question supplied by the teacher and styling it after the essays in the book review supplements of metropolitan newspapers. If preferred, the review can be an essay styled as literary criticism. The class can pretend it is writing a volume to be called "A Student Looks at Literature." Students are directed to use as many transitionary words as are sensible and practical to the logical development of their ideas and to underline them.

A five-member student committee chooses the five most successful essays and each committee member analyzes orally the reasons for the effectiveness of one review. They also choose the five least successful essays and in a symposium point out the weaknesses and suggest methods for improvement. A teacher may wish to mimeograph one of the unsuccesssful essays and ask the students to rewrite it, using the material of the original plus effective transitionary vocabulary to improve its quality.

#  Dear Diary

When students have completed a novel, they each take on the identity of one of its major or minor characters and write three entries of at least 150 words in the diary of that person. The entries need not be for successive days as they are to represent part of a complete diary maintained by the character to record the events of his life as revealed in the book. They should reflect the student's personal reactions to his character's involvement with some of the major plot episodes, his relationships with other characters, and an empathy with the moods, modes, and manners of the period of the novel. Sometimes an author makes these interpretations for the reader; more often he lets the reader piece them together for himself.

Naturally the writing will be most effective if its style typifies the character or in some cases reproduces the language of the time and locale of the novel. References to fellow characters as well as to plot details will breathe realism into the entries, which need not always adhere strictly to the stated plot line. For example, Lucie in *The Tale of Two Cities* could have written in her diary her reactions to some of the emotional and dramatic events associated with the freeing of her father from the Bastille or her personal reflections on some of the other events she witnessed. Becky in *Vanity Fair* could have kept a fascinating diary as her life was buffeted by people and events. Boys will determine that the Rev. Dimmesdale in *The Scarlet Letter* is a likely person to have kept a diary as is the introspective Heathcliff of *Wuthering Heights.*

Although these diary entries might seem on the surface to be shallow analyses of the reading, the teacher will recognize that the opposite is true. To impersonate a character, the reader must know the character; to live in a definite time, the reader must comprehend how plot is influenced by the forces of the period; to be a realistic part of a scene, the reader must be familiar with the locale.

The ready availability of paperbacks through book clubs and in bookstores makes it practical for two students to read the same novel if desired. After writing diary entries as described above, they can exchange their work and criticize each other's journal: Has the mood, atmosphere, and authenticity of the book been accurately re-created? Are the entries natural? Since the student critic is familiar with the book, he can write for his colleague a 50-75-word or more analysis of the strengths and weaknesses of the diary entries, and he can also correct mechanical errors in the composition. When this activity is shared by two students, there is communication, interaction, mutual understanding, and a common bond of helpfulness.

# 67 Guessing Game

After everyone has read a three-act play, novel, or collection of short stories, he writes a critique of one of the characters, the length being determined by grade and ability levels. Each character delineation begins with a similar topic sentence adapted to a student's individual need, e.g., "I was (repelled, absorbed, amazed, puzzled, inspired, informed, discouraged, delighted, astounded, shocked, disgusted, pleased, etc.) by one of the characters in my reading." He carefully avoids identifying either the character or the book but writes their names at the end of his piece. These sketches are read to the class by their writers, and the audience attempts to guess the names of the characters and the books. Listeners are expected to take notes somewhat in the form of an annotated bibliography.

After this round of talks, each student chooses to read one of the books that has just been reported upon by a classmate. He then writes a sketch about the same character previously considered but does not use the same topic sentence. Instead he supplies his own with the objective of challenging the interpretation given previously, concurring with and expanding the previous view, or adding new, more perceptive analyses of the character. Instead of reading these interpretations to the class, they are given to the students who originally reported the books. If the two students agree in their interpretations, no further action is necessary, but if there is disagreement, then the two students must confront each other orally, each defending his point of view while their classmates listen.

Besides all the obvious benefits derived from the method and manner of this activity, all students will be introduced to some leading characters from as many books as there are students in the class. That indeed is stretching their literary acquaintances efficiently and quickly!

# **68** I'll Quiz You

After a heterogeneous reading assignment or one limited to one type of literature, students are ready for a practical public speaking experience. The reading has been governed by one condition — that two students read the same book, after which each prepares ten questions about the volume. These queries must be fact-probing and thought-provoking. Five of the questions are written out and given to the partner, who will prepare the answers by making notes only. The remaining five questions will be placed in a sealed envelope with the name of the partner on it.

On an appointed day, each of the partners presents his prepared answers orally. Answering alternately lends variety. Then each student receives his envelope and gives impromptu answers, again each student alternating. Each partner is responsible for checking on correctness or incompleteness of answers. Occasionally they will disagree.

For some students with limited experience who dread a face-to-face confrontation with an audience, this kind of activity eases them gradually into more formal public speaking experiences. If the students sit at a table or desk and informally converse with each other, some of the more frightening aspects of the experience are eliminated.

# 69 Drama Festival

"The fifth period English 12 class of Miss Smith recently conducted a Drama Festival. Four mini-lectures were given by ———— on ———— on two successive days. A series of symposia held in the auditorium during two class periods to which Mr. Jones' and Miss Green's English 3 classes were invited, considered such subjects as ————, ————, and ————. Jane Smithers was the student coordinator for these events, assisted by Mark Mitchell who was the chairman of the final event, the presentation on the auditorium stage of four significant scenes chosen from the 30 plays that the students had read in preparation for the festival."

Such a news article might appear in the school newspaper if this activity were worked out to completion by a senior English class that had concentrated on drama for supplementary reading. The mini-lectures could be six 12-minute talks given on two successive days either in the auditorium or classroom. Students chosen for their speaking ability could plan with the coordinator and the teacher subjects that would be helpful to developing fuller appreciation of the drama. Drama textbooks as well as books of criticism and dramatic essays should be consulted to find appropriate topics. Treatment in the mini-lectures need not be extensive but purely of an introductory nature. Such topics as an examination of the various types of drama, how dramatic plots are built, how settings create atmosphere, what makes dramatic literature live, and other broad, general subjects make an excellent introduction to a drama festival.

The student coordinator makes a survey of the three-act dramas class members are reading and together with a committee, which he has appointed with the teacher as the adviser, divides the plays into some logical groupings of not less than six or more than ten. The categories might be American drama, contemporary drama, social dramas, the work of the great dramatists, or innumerable other possibilities.

These groups meet either within class or during an activity or club period to exchange information about their reading and prepare plans for a 20-minute symposium. The subject must be one that is broad enough to apply to all the dramas but specific enough to generate worthwhile commentary by the participants. Such subjects might be: The dramatist as a social critic; What is tragedy? — it's nature and implications; Why is drama difficult to read?; The drama of today compared to that of 25 years ago; Is drama realistic?; Is plot more important than characterization?; The art of the dramatist vs. the novelist; and Why plays survive from generation to generation. Of course 20 minutes are too short a time to treat any of these subjects with much depth, but, after all, students do not have the knowledge to consider them other than superficially, although some students may show amazing powers of perception if given the challenge to exhibit them. Each group elects a chairman to supervise the details of its symposium and to report to the coordinator. Everyone is assigned a subdivision of the symposium topic, and each prepares notes on 4 x 6 inch cards to expedite his oral presentation. All plays read must be brought into the discussion by the chairman. Speech textbooks or a lecture by the teacher can help students learn the techniques of conducting and participating in a symposium.

If plans are made well in advance, the final event can be a series of short scenes from some of the plays. Scenes involving just a few characters are wise choices. No sets are required, and only properties such as tables and chairs are necessary. A "walking rehearsal" technique is suggested in which the actors use scripts but are familiar enough with the action and dialogue to give convincing performances.

If a full-scale drama festival is possible, everything would be expanded in time and emphasis, with a more polished set of performances to conclude the project. The coordinator is all important because he must attend to the details of providing the table and chairs for the symposia, of inviting other English classes to attend, and above all of impressing upon each group chairman that each individual must prepare and participate in his symposium.

A large poster prominently displayed on the classroom bulletin board advertising the drama festival, the mini-lectures, and the symposia will give status to the program. The age level and maturity of the class will determine the depth and breadth of the festival, but one result is certain — the next play they read or see will be more deeply appreciated.

# 70 Drama Through the Ages

One approach to the study of drama is the historical. Books on the history of the theater discuss the eras of Greek, Roman, Italian (*commedia dell'arte*), Restoration, Elizabethan, and French drama and all the others in between and since. Although a detailed study of any one of these periods is not recommended for high school English courses, a general knowledge contributes to the cultural enrichment of students. A brief survey of the historical periods could be accomplished by:

1. A series of lectures by the teacher.
2. A series of lectures by students who have researched the periods.
3. A series of movies and filmstrips that explain and visualize the periods.

4. Records read by well-known artists who explain the historical periods.
5. Lectures by several teachers, with classes combined for a team teaching approach.
6. A combination of lecture and audio-visual materials.
7. An expert from outside the school talking on the subject.

Students, of course, take notes during these sessions. The class spends at least one period in the library where, guided by the teacher, the librarian, and any bibliographies provided by the latter, each student finds two plays representative of two different historical periods. Using both the background material of the lectures and their own intelligence, they are instructed to compare the two plays in five ways of their own choosing. The work will be done on sheets that have been divided vertically, with the comparisons and contrasts opposite each other. A prose style rather than a listing format is recommended.

The teacher will recognize this activity as one suitable for the college-bound, but its value should not be underrated for terminal students who have ability and need their cultural backgrounds strengthened by reading drama. Only the reluctant reader or the handicapped reader should never be expected to pursue this activity. Some kind of a summary day should develop from this reading so that ideas can be pooled, shared, argued, and compared.

# 71 The Masks of Comedy and Tragedy

The comedy of the Romans, the Italians' *commedia dell'-arte*, French comedy of Molière, British comedy, Shakespearean comedy, and contemporary comedy were and are very different from each other. In like manner, the tragedy of the Greeks differed considerably from that of Shakespeare and the avant-garde theater of today.

The various periods can be studied through research and reading, with individuals or small groups assigned to concentrate on two distinct periods of comedy or tragedy and report back to class orally. The teacher should request the librarian to put all books except the standard reference books on reserve to facilitate this work. Encyclopedias should not be overlooked, for their succinct summaries are often sufficient for the maturity of some classes. Many fine paperbacks are now available in fairly sturdy editions and can augment the conventional hard-cover collection. To find information some students will need help in using indices, tables of contents, and other aids.

During another library period, each student chooses two comedies or tragedies representative of two periods. After reading them, he writes an analysis of the differences in the nature of the comedy or tragedy of which each is an example. He uses the material he has researched or the information imparted to him by the students who reported to the class orally. A well-developed analysis should include three points of contrast. The teacher chooses the best papers covering each period and some of the better readers read them while the students take notes. Discussion should naturally follow.

# 72 Interviewing the Author

Younger students in grades seven through nine will enjoy the playacting possibilities of this activity, while senior high school young people will appreciate the creative and imaginative thinking involved in its execution.

Students must work as partners, and after reading the same novel or drama, one of the pair assumes the identity of the author and the other that of a reporter or interviewer. The reporter prepares his questions in advance on 3 x 5 inch cards. His questions may be similar to the following, although he will want to make them apply specifically to the book: As the author of this book, what would you consider the theme? What is the purpose of your book? Does it have a message? For whom did you write it? To whom is it important? Why did you choose this particular locale for the basic setting? Who do you consider the key character? Why? Why does the general subject of this writing appeal to you as an author? If he can find material on the book jacket or elsewhere about the author, the questioning at the end of the interview can relate to the author's life and work.

At the conclusion of this interview, the two partners take on new identities and conduct another interview for which they have prepared. The former reporter becomes one of the characters in the book, preferably the chief protagonist and the author becomes a student who has read the book and is interviewing the book personality. The questions will very likely take this trend: What other characters in the book influenced your actions and ideas? How? Why did you act or react in (specific situation from the book) as you did? Do you like your treatment by the author? How would you like to change your image in the eyes of the reader? Do you grow or develop in any specific way during the evolution of the plot? Do you degenerate? How? Do you think you will achieve any lasting fame in literature as a character of importance, or have you? Explain your answer. Do you think your author created you realistically? Explain.

Because this activity consumes considerable class time, only a limited number of students will participate, while the rest of the class will be assigned to a written activity.

117

# 73 The Play's the Thing

This activity will appeal to talented student writers who have a flair for creating and executing the dramatic form. The wise teacher will coordinate it with information about radio and television, two media closely allied with students' daily lives. Each student is to write a TV or radio script for a 30-minute dramatic performance if fiction has been read; if the reading was nonfiction, a documentary type of program is called for. Because this is to be written for educational television and radio, no commercial messages are to be included.

A committee of students works with the teacher to determine the winner of the first prize and the second and third runners-up. At least one winning script should be cast and produced by members of the class or members of the dramatic club, with the performance given for the English class of the student writer. This show could be "live" in the classroom or auditorium, or if the school has closed circuit television, it can be beamed to the class and others meeting during the same period. Careful supervision by the teacher will prevent an inordinate amount of time being spent preparing the program.

# 74 Best Sellers, Past and Present

The appearance of a title on a best seller list does not automatically mean that it has literary value, insure that it will maintain its popularity for all time, or even that it should be read immediately by those who wish to be informed, knowledgeable, or well read. Many other factors may be responsible for its rating. However, to insist that students' reading diets consist solely of the tried and approved books on the library shelves is also a fallacy. If students read only books they know have weathered the tests of time, they are not being trained to become discriminating readers. Therefore, this activity is concerned with best sellers, past and present.

Class members are sent on a massive hunt for best seller lists from newspapers and magazines. The school librarian may be able to supply lists of special interest to young people, as some of her professional journals concentrate on this age rather than adults. These sources are especially helpful if this activity takes place on a junior high school level. A committee can be designated to examine *The World Almanac* and similar fact and statistical books for lists of best sellers of previous years. *Seventy Years of Best Sellers* by Alice Payne Hackett (Bowker) and *Golden Multitudes: Best Selling Books* by Frank G. Mott (Bowker) contain a variety of lists and commentary plus references to other books and articles on the subject. Current lists as well as lists of best sellers of the past can be posted on the bulletin board or distributed to class members.

After this research, students write a one-page paper proposing three good reasons why books make best seller lists. One student may have read a magazine article on the subject, and he can summarize it orally for the class. In a short discussion period, class members can give their reasons for the popularity of certain books. A small committee can conduct a survey of school personnel and adults of their acquaintance, asking such questions as: How much of your reading is guided by best seller lists? In most instances, why do you think the average best seller achieves this importance? A report on this survey should produce provocative material for discussion.

The remainder of the activity may be carried out in six possible ways. The teacher can adopt the plan best suited to the needs and abilities of his class. All the plans, however, utilize the report form given at the end of this section.

1. Each student chooses a title from one of the lists, reads it, and fulfills the requirements for the report.

2. Students choose titles from a current week or month best seller list for fiction and general categories. In this case, more than one student will read the same book and various reactions will result.

3. As many students as there are titles on a current fiction or nonfiction list select a title, write a report, and prepare an oral summary for delivery to the class.

4. One student volunteers or is assigned to read the best selling fiction title that has been on a list for the longest number of weeks, and another reads the top nonfiction book. The two will then present a summary of their reactions using the report form in a dialogue format for their discussion.

5. Everyone in a row will read the same book chosen from the top five or six best sellers on a list. This is suggested for an older best seller for which paperback editions are available. After writing individual papers, each row conducts a forum-type discussion that brings out differing opinions and reactions.

6. Each student chooses two best sellers, one from the past five years and one from a previous period, preferably separated by five years or more. Using as much of the material from the report form as is appropriate, he compares the two books in as many ways as he honestly can.

Here is the suggested report form to duplicate and distribute to the class:

1. Make a list of all the reasons why this book may have made a best seller list.

2. If it is not from a current list, try to determine why it made the list in its day, remembering the history of that time. Why would it not be likely to be equally popular today, or is it?

3. If it is on a current list, predict its future popularity or obscurity.

4. Evaluate the chief virtues of the book, its main defects, and its importance in general.

5. Conclude with your personal reaction to the book, responding intelligently and sincerely.

If the teacher wishes any of these activities to conclude with oral summaries by small groups, the following questions might be posed: Are best sellers always wise, worthwhile, or desirable reading choices? What purposes do the lists serve? How are they determined? Is the appearance of an author's work on a list proof of anything? What? What best sellers of the past should students put on their "must read" lists? What best sellers should be in one's permanent library? What influence do national book clubs have on these lists? Is this good?

# 75 Story Time

After students have read either an anthology of short stories or an assortment from many sources, including magazines, each chooses one of the following ten plans and writes a paper on the short story as a form of literature, its importance, its characteristics, and its development. Because the short story and the one-act play have so many elements in common, the teacher can make the original assignment a combination of these two literary forms. The length of these analytical papers as well as the reading assignment depend upon the grade and ability level involved.

If the English course on the grade level for which this activity is being employed does not include a study of the short story or short drama, a research period should be spent in the library seeking information about exposition, characterization, plot lines, structure, climax, symbolism, and other facets of short stories and plays. Students and teachers can discover concrete assistance in analyzing short stories in *Reading, Understanding, and Writing About Short Stories* by H. Fenson and H. Kritzee (Free Press) and *Approaches to the Short Story* by N. D. Isaacs and L. Leiter (Chandler).

1. Apply four of the following essay questions to three stories, selecting different combinations for each analysis. Of course, some questions are more applicable to some stories than to others:

A. Setting. Does it contribute to the total effect? Is there unity of setting? Does it influence the plot? How? If not, to what element of the story does it contribute? If the major emphasis is the setting, sketch how this was treated by the author. Is it reminiscent of some other story read now or in the past? Expand this comparison.

B. Style. Does the writing style contribute in any special way to any aspects of the story or drama? Is it unique, simple, or complex? Explain. Is there unity of style? Prove general assertions with explanations. (If students need assistance to understand style and unity in the short story, they may need to do some research, or the teacher may discuss the characteristics of the short story form before the reading assignment is given.)

C. Point of view. From whose point of view was the story

related? How does the choice of narrator contribute to any one effect or the total effect? Show how the entire story could have been changed, improved, or ruined by using another narrator, citing a specific person to explain your thinking.

D. Structure. How does the story begin? Why was this technique used? What was the writer's plan? How effective is it? Where does the climax occur. Discuss its impact. Is it unexpected? Discuss. Briefly sketch the main events that produced the climax, explaining their significance in dictating either the climax or the end of the story.

E. Characterization. How was it achieved — through description, dialogue, other characters, or a combination? Was the method of creating characters the same for all or were different means used? Discuss two characters to illustrate.

F. Theme. Does the story or drama have a theme? What is it? Is the theme important to you? If not, to whom? Do you agree with its premise or philosophy?

G. Do you honestly like the story? What was its attraction? If it annoyed, displeased, repulsed, or otherwise adversely affected you, explain your reaction in detail.

H. Recommendation. To whom will the story appeal? Do not generalize but express in specific terms.

2. These questions should be applied to as many stories as the teacher has assigned:

A. Does the story contain symbolism? Explain in detail giving illustrations. Why was it used? What contribution does it make? If it is a subtle use rather than an obvious one, explain why the author chose this technique. What does the symbolism contribute to the story?

B. Does irony play a part in plot, setting, characterization, theme, climax, or denouement? Explain.

C. What purposes do digressions serve if they are employed?

D. Are the plot, characters, theme, setting, and other elements plausible? Explain.

E. How is suspense achieved? What purpose did it serve?

F. Choose the outstanding feature of each story and specifically describe how it made an impact on the story and subsequently on the reader.

3. Characters are revealed through exposition, dialogue, actions and reactions, and outright descriptions by the author and other characters. Write a study of how characterization was developed in each story assigned, preferably at least three.

4. Some stories lean heavily on theme; in others it is barely perceptible. State the themes of at least five stories as succinctly as possible, then explain their significance for the characters. Present your personal reactions to three themes, agreeing or disagreeing with them according to your own experience, personality, or philosophy.

5. Atmosphere is employed to enhance the action, characters, theme, or plot. Choose three stories and develop a detailed examination of the contribution of atmosphere to the technical fabric of short stories. A study of dialogue and its contribution to three stories or the importance of plot may be substituted for atmosphere.

6. Endings are of many types, depending upon the immediate purpose of the author. Referring to five completely different endings, write a personal analysis of their variations, purposes, results, and other aspects such as plausibility, inevitability, justification, or ridiculousness. You may also consider the current trend of the "no end" story that defines the conclusion vaguely or leaves it in limbo for the reader to supply according to his own understanding of the story or of life in general.

7. Using at least three stories but more if necessary, write an analytical paper on the minor characters. Touch upon their function and utilization by the author, by other characters, and by the plot. Illustrate with examples.

8. Support the contention that people in short stories neither think nor act like their counterparts in real life situations. Refer to as many stories as you have read to make your paper convincing.

9. Write your intellectual reactions to five stories rather than analyzing them. Discuss the type of reader who would enjoy or find satisfaction in reading them. Three reasons for or against each story should be proposed to give the arguments weight and conviction.

10. Write a paper on the significance and importance of titles, referring to the titles of ten specific stories to support your generalizations.

#  On Record

After reading dramas, poetry, classical novels, or biographies of poets, playwrights, musicians, or famous contemporary personages, a few students can present novel oral reviews by utilizing the records and recording equipment available in the school. Catalogs in the library, centralized audio-visual department, or in the music, history, or English departments can be checked to see if there are records that contain poems by the poet whose biography or autobiography has been read, poems read by the poet himself, music by the composer whose biography has been read, excerpts from the play read, excerpts from the novel read, or voices of famous people such as Kennedy, Churchill, or Roosevelt if their biographies have been read.

Four or five students each prepare an outline for a ten-minute presentation on their reading, employing excerpts from the records to elaborate on, illustrate, or explain points made in their critiques. These should be well organized and appropriate to the commentary, not just a series of disjointed recordings. Since several records might be used, which could cause delays and awkward breaks, the excerpts can be taped in sequence ahead of time to provide smoother synchronization of the critical and audio material, or another student who has practiced with the speaker could operate the record player.

# 77 Aspects of the Novel

This activity is intended for an average class that needs direction to increase the depth and scope of its reading or for upperclassmen who need the additional experience in reading with understanding and perception. Two specific books are recommended for this concentrated study of the novel form, but there are many other excellent volumes that can help students develop quality reading appreciation (see Selected Sources).

In 1927 the British writer E. M. Forster delivered a series of lectures at Trinity College, Cambridge, which have been published with the title *Aspects of the Novel*. Available in both hard cover and paperback (both published by Harcourt, Brace and World), it has become a classic guide for in-depth study of the novel. Students can study Forster's work in one of four ways:

1. If there are enough copies for each student, the teacher can devise his own method of study.
2. Order as many copies as there are chapters, namely nine. One student can be responsible for summarizing and explain-

ing the theories projected by Forster in each chapter. These nine students can be boys and girls interested in English and perhaps intending to become English majors in college.

3. Two students can be assigned to read each chapter and to present an oral summary in the form of a dialogue that brings out the important contentions.

4. Several English classes can meet together in a large lecture room or in the auditorium, and the teachers can cooperate in lecturing about the book, summarizing, explaining, and illustrating the main points according to the maturity of the students involved. The material can be redigested later in individual classes for those who have questions. These points, among others, are advanced by Forster: the fundamental element of the novel is the story, the second aspect is people, and they are not like people in real life, plots in novels are not chronological as events in life are, and fantasy must be accepted by readers.

After studying *Aspects of the Novel*, each student reads two novels that are very different in style, subject, or other characteristics and develops a paper comparing the two works according to at least three of Forster's aspects. All generalizations must be explained, and all terms defined. One way to proceed is to divide the paper vertically down the middle and write about the first aspect of one novel on the left side and of the second novel on the right side, and so on. An undivided page will be used for the conclusions the students reach as they evaluate their reading by Forster's criteria.

*The Art of Reading the Novel* by Phillip Freund (Collier, Macmillan) is a perceptive study of the major works of Fielding, Melville, Hardy, Conrad, Lawrence, Proust, Virginia Woolf, and others. Each student skims through the book and chooses an author and book for concentrated study. He reads one of the novels discussed in detail and then writes a précis of Freund's commentary and his personal reactions to the book and Freund's treatment of it.

# 78 Extending Horizons

When a student enters the English classroom, he brings his interests in science, math, music, art, history, business, or other curriculum areas with him. Vocational choices can develop from these interests as students mature, and reading, writing, and speaking skills can be nurtured by assigning supplementary reading based on them.

Some students may select subjects in which they are not currently taking courses but which represent vocational fields that have special attractions for them. Books on religion, psychology, sociology, and the advanced sciences would fall in this category. The reading is climaxed by the preparation and delivery of five-minute speeches, which may employ audio devices to embellish, explain, or illustrate the subject matter. Because of time limitations, probably only part of the class can participate in the speaking activity; the others can prepare written reports.

Although no one outline can meet the requirements of all subject fields, this general guide for speech content is suggested:

1. What is the basic purpose of the author, either as he states it or as the reader determines it?
2. What is the scope of the subject matter?
3. Does the book accidentally or purposefully destroy old images and prejudices or create new concepts?
4. What is its most startling contribution?
5. Why is it a significant book, or isn't it?
6. In some detail, explain some of the topics explored.
7. Choose one chapter or section that was of particular interest and summarize it and its appeal.
8. Is the book for the layman, the specialist, the hobbyist, the expert, or the casual reader? Explain.

It is the teacher's responsibility to help students realize that broad areas such as home economics can be broken down into smaller specialties such as nutrition and that history can be divided into periods, art into schools of technique, and music into eras or trends. A boy or girl who is genuinely fascinated by a relatively narrow subject can bring new information and understanding to his classmates, and both speaker and audience will benefit. The outstanding talks can be recommended to specific departments in the school for delivery to classes where the content would be meaningful. Written reports could be submitted to the subject area teacher. Dovetailing projects such as this make students realize that the skills learned in English classrooms are realistic and practical.

 **Buy Our Books**

Pamphlets and brochures issued by national book clubs to advertise future selections must first be collected from family, friends, faculty, and students. They usually contain one long review of the book being promoted as the monthly choice; alternate options are described in shorter paragraphs. The brochures need not be current nor cover up-to-date selections; pamphlets used by previous classes can be reused just as new contributions can be saved for future classes.

Before distributing the material, the teacher should write some thought-provoking questions on the blackboard: What techniques are employed in this type of review? What part does psychology play? Is there appeal to status, prejudice, or other emotion? What emphasis is placed on plot, characters, readability, immediacy, sensationalism, the author's reputation, or availability? Each student examines as many reviews as possible during a class period, taking notes prompted by the questions as well as any personal reactions he may have. If the supply of pamphlets is meager, they may be projected for group examination. After a sufficient number have been analyzed, the teacher leads a discussion of the findings and conclusions. Again visual projection may be employed if there is disagreement or doubt on any points brought up. Characteristics of this type of book review should be well defined and recorded by the students in their notebooks or on a ditto stencil by a secretary.

After completing a supplementary reading assignment, students write a review for a book club brochure published by an existing book club or an imaginary one. Preferably the brochure should be illustrated, but if a student has no artistic talent, he can paste in illustrations from magazines. Two students may work together if they assume that a dual selection is being offered and two reviews are appropriate.

Some aspects of critical reviewing are, of course, sacrificed as these reviews are obviously slanted in complete approbation of a book, but students can learn valuable lessons about colorful, forceful, entertaining, and economic writing. The wise teacher will include a study of the vocabulary skills of professional copywriters to impress students with the importance of developing and enlarging upon this basic writing tool.

# 80 Take Your Choice

The three parts of this activity are designed for small groups within a class, with the assumption that the remaining students will learn from listening.

1. Three or possibly four students read different biographies about the same person and prepare individual five-minute talks primarily on the methods the biographers used to reveal their subject. The result will be that the biographee will emerge as a quite different personality according to the variations in emphasis or the prejudices of the biographers. During the remaining class time the speakers conduct a symposium, defending or criticizing the authors, evaluating their books in terms of the other biographies, and giving the audience an understanding of the biographee as well as of the art and skill of the biographers. The group can use excerpts from recordings of the voice of the biographee if they are available. As a bonus, the participants could issue an annotated bibliography of all the books in the school and class libraries about the biographee. The secondary purpose of this type of report is to motivate reading among the listeners.

2. Individual students speak for about five minutes on a book read for supplementary reading and then distribute to the class quickie-quizzes based on the material in the talk. The accuracy of the answers to his objective test will help the speaker recognize his weaknesses or strengths in promoting and explaining ideas to an audience; listeners will be jarred into improving their listening skills if the results of the test are poor. All grade levels enjoy this activity, but the length of the speeches and the quality of the quizzes will vary with the maturity of the students. The teacher may wish to delay the quizzes until all the speeches have been delivered or may even postpone them until a future period to test the retention powers of the audience.

3. All class members conduct research on the lives of the authors of their books and write a profile in the first person, including references to the book and to experiences that may have influenced his writing it, the subject matter, characters, events, theme, or even the style. A student committee, working with the teacher, will select the ten best profiles. Each "author," seated with his nine "colleagues" before the class,

will read or better yet talk spontaneously about himself. Five members of the audience, picked by the committee or the teacher for their intelligence and aggressiveness, then become a truth squad. They will be prepared to question the "authors" about themselves and their work and to elicit more opinions and information about the books read.

# 81 Author Meets the Critics

Adult readers usually develop preferences in authors either through habit or a genuine regard for their talents. This familiarity often provides greater depth of appreciation, although a wise reader does not limit himself to a few authors.

A committee of three students prepares the details of a class session held in the library during which all possible sources for researching authors will be explored and explained. One student can exhibit the reference books, while their nature and use is described by a student "teacher." The instructor serves as an adviser, correcting erroneous ideas or augmenting scanty information. The listeners take notes about the books and their locations in the library and can spend another profitable class period inspecting personally these sources. They will discover that some references give only basic data while others contain background material on the author's life and times, his place in the literary period of which he was a member, his characteristics as a writer or critic, what critics have said about him, and criticisms of specific works he has written.

Each student chooses an author, two of whose books he can locate. Before beginning the reading, he researches the writer. Perhaps two long and three short references would be the minimum assignment, but the greater the depth and scope of the research, the more successful the activity will be. Full biographies and monographs, for instance, should not be overlooked. Upon completing the reading, each student writes a paper revealing how the books are representative of the author in the light of the research conducted on him.

Points to consider might be: What are the characteristics of his writing? What were his ambitions or aims for himself as a writer? Did he succeed? Were the two books different or similar? How? What is the basic style and did it change in the two books? Explain. Did he belong to a school or tradition of writing? Does he remind you of another author? What part did his real life experiences play in his writing? Did social situations influence his work? Did other writers with whom he was acquainted influence him? Can the man be separated from the author? What are your personal reactions to the books, favorable and unfavorable? Would you want to read more works by him? Defend the stand taken. Evaluate the method of researching an author before reading his books. In this latter analysis, students should not be complimentary to flatter the teacher nor prejudiced to justify their lack of enthusiasm, but as honest as possible to determine the values and defects of the method.

Five students are then chosen by the teacher or by lot or elected by their classmates to assume the identities of the authors whom they have researched and whose works they have read. Five other groups of three students each will act as critics. Each group of critics plans an intelligent set of questions to pose to the author assigned to them. The teacher will probably wish to assist these groups in shaping worthwhile questions, which are not revealed to the "authors" ahead of time, although they could be given one or two questions for which they can prepare answers before an "Author Meets the Critics" session. If well planned, all five authors may be interviewed in one period, but so much interest may be generated that the encounters will need to spill over to another period, which can be concluded with general discussion and evaluation.

This author-in-depth treatment gives everyone, participants and listeners, more information about the world of books and authors.

# 82 Statements! Statements!

Each student writes a series of statements about a book he has read for pleasure. They can be isolated comments and need have no relationship to each other. They must not contain the name of the book or its author, although both are identified at the end of the statements. After arranging the desks and chairs in a circle or square, each boy or girl reads his statements but withholds the name of the title and the author, giving his classmates an opportunity to guess them, thus creating an attention-getting device to maintain audience interest. Because some students are not psychologically or intellectually capable of formal public speaking unless eased into it gradually through progressive steps, this activity is one method of preparing less aggressive students to perform for an audience, even one as well known as their own class.

A variation of this activity involves a type of writing practice that emphasizes the progression and flow of ideas. During a class session, or writing workshop as the teacher may prefer to call it, students write about the reading they have just enjoyed. It may be factual comment or opinions or personal reactions. They are instructed to write constantly for 15 minutes, writing first a statement, then expanding and explaining it until the subject is exhausted, then adding another general idea and proceeding in the same manner until the time limit is up. The statements need not follow each other logically. This type of writing exercise has proved to be a good device to develop fluency in composition. Later the logical progression can be incorporated into the writing, but until fluency is established as a habit, students are not capable of logical development. After the writing session, students read their work and underline five of the most significant points made. These may be sentences, phrases, or in some instances single words. An oral exchange follows, with each student sharing his commentary with his classmates. Reluctant readers especially will welcome the de-emphasis on the report itself.

# 83 Let's Have an Argument

Providing an opportunity for students to argue constructively is the keynote of this activity. Exchanging conflicting ideas stimulates original thinking and honest appraisal of the other fellow's opinions.

After reading a book of his own choice, each student prepares a brief argumentative speech beginning with one of the following exhortative statements:

1. All boys (girls) in (junior, senior) high school should read (name of book).
2. All (grade level) students should read (name of book).
3. All students who (insert condition) should read (name of book).

Students who wish to insert the word "not" after "should" may do so. Some excellent thinking has been done by students defending negative ideas when everyone else is being positive. Some students may have selected the wrong book, and they should be encouraged to express opinions.

All the talks must have three clearly defined reasons backed up with specific examples. Students may use any tactic they desire, and usually the challenge of an opportunity to be completely honest stimulates better preparation and interest than an assignment designed to please the teacher. Students must learn to be discerning readers, approving or rejecting just as adults do. In fact, if none of the suggested statements receive their approval, they should be allowed to formulate their own.

While the speeches are being delivered, the audience takes notes on the three arguments projected and makes short comments on whether they are logical, justified, too general, ridiculous, or poorly developed. After a talk, the class should be given the opportunity to challenge the speaker. This question period may have to be limited to one minute, with a student timekeeper in charge, as all the other student speakers must be heard. No one will find this type of review boring, and all will be introduced to a nodding acquaintance with more books and authors and have a chance to practice some logical thinking and some public speaking.

# 84 Style? What's That?

The word "style" in composition and literature is usually a mystifying and misunderstood term among students because authorities and textbooks differ widely in their definitions. The dictionary explanation that style is a way of expressing oneself in language, manner, or appearance is too broad to clarify the concept, and even the thesaurus fails to list words that aid understanding. This activity will not dispel all the confusion students have about style in writing, but if it is painstakingly conducted with much augmentation by the teacher, repeated exposure can make a breakthrough.

A committee of students can investigate books on composition and literary criticism techniques in the library as well as look in *Readers' Guide to Periodical Literature* for references to current or past articles on style. The teacher will probably want to add to the list the committee compiles before it is dittoed for the entire class, and he will certainly want to make sure it includes the widely used *The Elements of Style* by William Strunk, Jr., and E. B. White (Macmillan, paperback). The assignment will be to read a required number of pages from the list. For practical purposes limit the study to eleventh- and twelfth-grade students.

Several periods of discussion will logically follow during which students can suggest their answers to the question, What is style? The range of different opinions students will have encountered will make the resolution of their ideas into a capsule generalization difficult. There will be conflicting opinions as a definition evolves gradually on the blackboard, so the process should be unhurried to permit full discussion of divergent findings. Although the following is not intended to be a definitive definition of the nature of style, it does represent an example of the type of statement students and teacher can eventually create:

"Style can be considered: (1) expressing oneself honestly with (2) clarity, (3) brevity, and (4) respect for the reader, not to confuse him but to aid his comprehension. Added to these characteristics are (5) variety, (6) good humor, (7) good sense, (8) vitality, and (9) imagination. Variety implies avoiding monotonous language and sentence structure; metaphors and similes inject vitality and imagination and keep the language lively. In summary, (10) ideas must be clear and (11) basic expression simple, although this does not infer that simplicity cannot be powerful."

Examples of good style can be introduced by way of illustration, and class members can be instructed to find their own samples of effective writing styles. Their response will indicate if the teacher was successful in explaining this elusive aspect of composition and if students recognize the characteristics of style. The study can culminate with writing a critique on a recently read book, emphasizing the author's style with references to the main points in the class's general statement on style. The best analyses can be shared with the class. To promote the development of individual style, the teacher may wish to schedule several writing workshop sessions in which composition skills are stressed.

# 85 Armchair Travel

With advances in communication making even remote areas of the world more accessible, with social and economic problems demanding solution through a world community of nations, and with military confrontations flaring constantly in different parts of the globe, it is unfortunate that the average student ignores the travel section of the library, thus missing the opportunity to add to his understanding of areas far removed from his daily life but with an effect on it. Even reading the front page of a newspaper would be more meaningful if supported by background reading of this type.

No longer is the travel book only an account of some brave explorer's dangerous ride down the Colorado River, although happily many wonderful books of this type are still being written and read, but this category includes commentaries not only on places but on the people, their past and present history, their problems, their needs, and their contributions. Too often the history or English teacher has to assign this type of reading or it is neglected. This activity includes four suggestions for using travel books to break down prejudices and widen students' personal and world horizons.

1. The theme for the reading can be "An Armchair Trip Around the World." Each student is directed to read at least one book that deals with actual travel experiences or considers political, social, or economic conditions of a country. He then writes an article to be submitted to an imaginary magazine called *Travelogue*. His thesis will be that his ideas have been expanded by the book, and he will try to create reader interest by writing in an informative and entertaining way. The best articles may be read aloud.

2. With a "Know America First" theme, the teacher will list on the blackboard students' suggestions of some of the important areas of the United States, including its immediate neighbors if desired. Each student locates and reads a book about one of the regions on the list and writes a 300-word entry for a contest sponsored by *America the Beautiful*, a fictitious magazine. The objective is to prove how reading can help one understand America better and create a better informed citizenry.

3. Social studies teachers often require senior students to read books that treat the socio-economic or the socio-political situations of other countries and areas. Each student selects such a volume and after reading it writes a 300-word dissertation on why he is now wiser, more knowledgeable, and better oriented as a world citizen. He is to imagine that this is a speech he has been asked to deliver to a tenth-grade history class to persuade the younger students to begin the habit of reading this type of book. An extra sheet of blank paper can be attached to the end of each essay, and during a class read-

ing session the proposed speeches can be exchanged. Each reader records his reactions on the blank sheet, commenting briefly on the essay's weaknesses and strengths, its fallacies and truths, and its effectiveness for the purpose for which it was written.

4. Each student prepares a brief talk using the material of a travel book but not revealing the name of the people or country. After his speech, the audience attempts to identify the geographical location. Some books are more appropriate for this type of report than others, so an alternative is to identify the area and have the speaker distribute a brief dittoed quickie-quiz requiring true-false or multiple choice answers. When he corrects the tests he will learn if he was an effective speaker, while the class will learn if they were careful listeners.

# 86 Amateur Dramatics

If the ability level of the class warrants, a teacher may wish to attempt some original dramatics by presenting key scenes from well-known novels. Several plans are possible:

1. Divide into small groups, each of which reads novels by one author such as Dickens, Hemingway, Brontë or Faulkner.
2. Everyone in the class reads novels by one author.
3. Everyone in the class reads a novel by any well-known author.
4. Only one small group of eight-ten students concentrate on one novelist, reading at least four or five of his works.

As students read, they note episodes that could be easily rewritten as dramatic scenes. Each group discusses possible scenes and jointly writes and produces a play using simple props either in classroom or auditorium settings. If the assignment has involved the entire class, a general discussion is held with everyone making suggestions. A committee then works out the details of preparing one or two dramatic scenes for a performance.

Students can also produce a lasting memento of their ingenuity by typing and binding a book entitled "Scenes from (novelist's name)." Another composition by-product could be writing magazine articles for submission to a magazine subscribed to by English teachers. Its purpose would be to explain how the class prepared and presented this technique of reporting on novels. Possible titles might be: "How Dickens Visited Our Class," "Scenes from the Classics," "On Stage with Hemingway," "Curtain Calls for Willa Cather," or "Dramatic Moments from Great Novels." If any student does write an article that has quality, the teacher may actually submit it to an education magazine to prove to the students that English class activities, oral and written, are practical, purposeful, and rewarding.

# 87 Creative Comparisons

Boredom with book reports stems from the repetitious nature of the assignment and from the absence of challenge in their substance. Comparisons stimulate creative thinking, and analysis compels students to produce ideas and to defend them. Young minds can be trained to observe, weigh, and evaluate the conclusions they reach. Because needs and abilities vary with individual students and classes as a whole exhibit divergent ambitions and background, a dozen plans are suggested for this activity to meet all capabilities. Most of the plans are associated with nonfiction reading, but a few pertain to novels, drama, and biography.

1. Choose a country, a continent, or a region (not the United States) and read a nonfiction book published ten or more years ago about that area and a very recent book, written preferably within the last two years, on the same general locality. Write a comparative analysis of differences in the authors' presentations, that is the style, attitudes, material, background knowledge, readability, pertinence, effectiveness, or opinion-shaping techniques and summarize the differences, major and minor, in the people and the development or problems of the country during the years between the two publications.

2. Read Thoreau's *Walden*, or extensive excerpts from it, then read a book by a modern nature writer such as Joseph Krutch or Rachel Carson. Write a comparative analysis of the two works, bringing out at least three similarities and three differences and using the format of a magazine article for an imaginary magazine, *Woods and Dells*, whose readers are nature lovers and conservationists.

3. Read a novel or a biography written during the Victorian era and a novel or biography published within the past 25 years, then write an analysis comparing the two in ten different ways.

4. Read two novels about two different wars and write a comparative analysis of the treatment of the subject by each author, including as many points as necessary to be convincing.

5. Choose two areas of the world that are critical from an economic or political point of view, a nonfiction book about each, and write a comparative analysis of the situations re-

sponsible for the problems or crises. A summary of each book is not sufficient; comparisons of the opinions and presentations of the two authors are required.

6. An individual or a group of students choose a specific period, such as 19th-century England, the American Expansion Era, Post-World War II, or the Depression, or a literary trend, such as the psychological novel or even current avant-garde literature, and read some basic background material prior to reading two works of fiction representative of the period or the trend. An interesting variation would be to read one work by a woman author and one by a man. A comparative analysis of the techniques of each author and of the influences of the times in which he wrote can be composed, with references to the contributions each made to literature.

7. Each student or a small group reads one novel by a foreign author and one by an American author and writes an analysis of the two volumes, comparing them in as many ways as possible for balance and comprehension. Some valuable discussion periods could develop from this.

8. A student who would be challenged by depth-in-reading can choose two psychological novels, one written in the 1920's and one of current vintage. He might even like to read a third very early example such as a Henry James novel. As capably as his perceptions will permit, he writes a comparative analysis of the development of the psychological novel. Undoubtedly he will need to do some preliminary research in books of literary criticism.

9. After reading two historical novels, a student compares them in any way he wishes, but for genuine development, a minimum of three to five ways is suggested.

10. With the assistance of his teacher and from suggestions of his classmates, each student chooses two dissimilar authors, for example Arnold Bennett and John Dos Passos or Daphne du Maurier and John Steinbeck and reads an example of the work of each. The two opposites will furnish material for a

comparative analysis of the student's reactions to the subjects, characters, styles, and philosophies, and their effects upon him.

11. After reading a time-tested play and a recognized novel, e.g., a Cather novel and an O'Neill play, students write a comparative analysis, drawing upon material specifically suggested by the reading to develop their points and reactions to the methods and motivations of each writer.

12. A student who is particularly interested in biography can be guided by his teacher to do research tracing the development of biographical writing through the memoir and diary stages, the complimentary era that treated the biographies unrealistically, and up to today's frank and often debunking approaches that are designed to be sensational but in most cases strive to be honest and realistic. After reading at least one biography of each type, the student writes an analytical comparison showing the advantages and disadvantages of each technique, plus his own conclusions.

The teacher will recognize that all these assignments can be expanded into term papers whenever student enthusiasm develops. Class discussions based on the comparisons would seem to be another natural outgrowth of the program.

 **Guest Speakers**

This activity suggests some unique formats for reporting orally on book reading assignments.

1. Oral book talks can be delivered to other English classes

meeting the same period. Perhaps an exchange day could be arranged during which all the English classes in the school entertain guest book reviewers. The speakers need not be restricted to their own grade level — seniors can visit sophomores and juniors can visit freshmen classes. However, a talk is more successful if a speaker does not address a group older than himself, which decrees that seventh graders speak to each other or entertain guest reviewers. Some students may wish to practice within their own classes; others who have given fine reviews for their classes on some previous occasion may be chosen for exchange book review day.

2. A forum or discussion group that has proved its ability could also present a book discussion for another class that meets during the same period; the grade level need not be the same. A variation could be for two students from one class to engage in a book discussion with two members of a host class, if the four will cooperate in some way on the original reading. A tape of the discussion can be made to bring the exchange to the class from which the visitors came.

3. An author in the area can be a guest speaker for a combined session of all English classes. After reading some of his books, students can report how they substantiated the remarks made by the author himself. If a visit by an author is imposible to arrange, perhaps a responsible student can interview a local writer and give his class a summary, after which books by the author would be read.

4. A group of eight-ten students who have read nonfiction books can invite two or three teachers who do not have scheduled classes during the period the English class meets to quiz the group on its reading. The teachers are given a list of the books ahead of time to permit them to prepare, and they are requested to ask probing questions that will reveal the subject matter to the audience and the value of the works to the average reader.

5. Each student prepares five good questions of a general nature applicable to any biography, novel, drama, or other type of book read by class members. The teacher collects the questions, which have been written on five separate sheets, and evaluates their point value for a quiz game. The questions are placed in separate boxes labeled with the point values, and the class is divided into four teams. The first student decides the point value he wishes to try for, e.g., 25, 50, 75, or 100 points, and a question is selected and read by a master of ceremonies who is a non-contestant. Teammates may help only in making a choice of the score to aim for; they cannot assist in answering a question. The contestant must apply his question to his own reading. The teacher and two student judges decide whether to award the points. Scorekeepers can occasionally post team scores. The winning team certainly deserves a round of soft drinks later, courtesy of all the losers.

# 89 Bibliographies

A form of book promotion that is probably familiar to students although they may not recognize it as promotion is the monthly bibliography issued by librarians in some schools to interest the students in both new and old books. Using such a bibliography as the model, the teacher arranges a writing workshop in a class period. Students are not told the details in advance except that everyone who can contribute thesauri, books of synonyms, or dictionaries is asked to do so. When these are added to those the teacher supplies, there should be enough to go around. Each student is to write continuously for 20 minutes anything he wishes about his reading. The writing will flow without any predetermined plan or outline; some students will concentrate on one aspect, while others will digress into several channels of thought. The idea is to keep writing until the end of the assigned time. A wise plan is to divide the paper vertically, using the right side for this preliminary writing.

At the conclusion of the time limit, the second direction is given. Each student is to compress his original writing into a 25-30-word summary that would be suitable in a bibliography such as those the librarian or her staff prepare on many occasions for teachers' and students' use. The secret is to include as much of the original material as possible by condensing whole sentences and paragraphs into one and two words. Hence the need for the thesauri and dictionaries. The left side of the paper can be used as a work sheet in this condensing. The final condensation under a title and author citation will be written on another paper and submitted with all the preliminary work. In a succeeding period, before the teacher evaluates them, the summaries can be circulated around the class with each student reading as many as possible and writing unsigned comments about their effectiveness on the back of the papers. Typical comments might be: "What do you mean by the vague word 'interesting'?" or "Your sentence concentrates on too limited an aspect of the book!"

Practical use can be made of these bibliographical annotations; for example they can be combined under an appropriate heading such as "Books Teenagers Are Reading," mimeographed, and distributed to this and other English classes. If this is impractical, all the condensations could be presented to the librarian with the expectation that she might use the best of them in some future monthly bulletin or in some specific bibliography requested by a teacher.

# 90 Points of View

Sometimes students fail to recognize that some books were originally written in a language other than English and are translations or they avoid such books because they are unfamiliar with the settings or situations. They thus lose the opportunity to learn about people of other nations through their own men of letters. For example, novels written by Asiatics give insights into the peoples and philosophies of the East that no Occidental writer could convey.

An interesting project is to read a translated work and in a 300-word critique show how it revealed a different way of life, a new social or political or ethical philosophy, an unfamiliar set of mores or behavior patterns, or a world quite different from that of the reader and writer of the analysis. Currently the need to understand not only nations and emerging continents but also the ethnic and racial groups within our own country is being stressed. A variation of this activity can be to read literature emanating from these ethnic groups, with emphasis on the contributions of Negro writers, past and present. Groups within the class could concentrate on one ethnic group by researching its literature, reading it, and presenting oral summaries of their findings. Naturally students who belong to that ethnic background should be in the group, with their parents or grandparents assisting them in locating some of the literature. Anthologies of world literature are excellent sources.

This entire reading project could, with proper motivation from the teacher and an enthusiastic response by the students, develop into an international literature festival within the classroom, and create new appreciation for the cultural backgrounds of fellow students who are different in race or nationality.

# 91 Dear Sir

Letter writing affords a variety of informal ways to report on supplementary reading. Each student can write a letter to the author of a book he has just read telling him what aspect of it impressed him most, its value to him, a comparison with other books by the same writer, if known, or other frank but just commentary. Of course the letters will not be mailed as authors are too busy to be bombarded with letters from young America. However, the letters will make an interesting bulletin board display, especially if photographs of the authors and a display of their works are included.

The class could imagine that a high school book club is anxious to receive suggestions from students for possible future selections, and negative or positive recommendations of not less than 150 words can be addressed to the editor of the club and his board of advisers. Again these letters should not be mailed as clubs have their own methods for determining selections. The most comprehensive and best composed letters can be read aloud.

A third and very realistic variation is for everyone to read a book that is not in the school library. This fact can be ascertained by checking the card catalog. Paperbacks found in local bookstores might be a source of the reading. Each class member writes a letter to the school librarian either recommending that his book be purchased for the library or complimenting her on her good judgment for not purchasing it. In both instances the general statements must be backed up with specific reasons and references. These letters could be passed along to the librarian, although further study would be wise before specific suggestions are made. Perhaps several other students could at least skim a book before a definite purchase request is submitted to the library staff.

# 92 Giants of the Literary World

The teacher will probably want to preface this activity with an introduction to some of the greatest writers throughout history. They may be limited to the greats in one literary category, such as the novel or drama, but an equally effective study can be conducted with mixed categories represented by such writers as Shakespeare, Arnold Bennett, Hemingway, Chekhov, Austen, Dumas, Molière, Faulkner, Ibsen, and many others. The information given would of necessity not be comprehensive but of a general nature, for some of these names, or those the teacher selects, will be unknown to some students.

The notes students take during these lectures will help them select an author whom they wish to know more about both as a person and as an author. All possible biographical and critical sources should be examined, and during a class session in the library the nature of the resource materials and their use can be explained. Some requirement on the number of sources to be explored will probably be given before students are assigned to write thumbnail biographies. When his sketch is complete, a student reads two works by his author and writes a longer summary of how his background, family, education, avocations, philosophy, or other factors revealed in the research influenced his writing in any ways that were discernible. Some oral discussion in which class members share the latter paper should be arranged.

A variation is to concentrate not on the authors but on the characters they created. For instance, all the girls in the class can combine their efforts to present an oral program on famous women in fiction. Each girl, with the advice of her teacher, can discover a famous female character, read the book of which she is the heroine, and write a summary of her life. To make the biographical sketch more realistic, a girl can imagine that a movie is being planned for her book and that she is on the production staff. Her sketch of the woman, based on her careful reading of the book, will guide the casting director, the costume designer, and others who must make decisions wherever this character is involved. No limit can be placed on length, as the variations and ramifications of fictional characters are too great.

# **93** Books That Changed the World

One of the following paperbacks will be needed to develop this activity: *Thirty-Five Best Sellers of the Ages* by James O'Donnell Bennett (Fawcett), which contains brief summaries and discussions of 35 books and their appeal for readers, or *Books That Changed the World* by Robert B. Downes (New American Library), which analyzes the content and influence of 16 lasting works. The same plan can be applied to both volumes, but the books covered in the latter represent more difficult reading. Other titles of this nature may be found in paperback listings, catalogs, or visits to well-stocked bookstores.

The teacher divides the class into small groups of five members each, using his discretion to include a mixture of abilities and ambitions; each group is given at least three copies of the Bennett or Downes book. Students will want a theme for this activity, such as "Books That Changed Minds," "Great Books," "Books That Will Live Forever," or "Books for

Thinking Men and Women." The small committees will examine the books and decide which titles suggested by these men as must reading they will each read, making sure they do not duplicate choices within the group, although there will be duplication within the class. Each committee decides upon some oral format to discuss its books — individual speeches, forum, symposium, or a debate. The objective is to familiarize their classmates with as many great books as possible. Deviation from the material presented by Downes and Bennett, of course, is to be expected and hoped for if the activity is successful.

# 94 In Manuscript Form

Students are instructed to imagine that the book they have just read is still in manuscript form and has not been published, although obviously the contrary is true. Each assumes the identity of a manuscript reader employed by a large publishing company. Every week he and the other readers of new manuscripts report to the editor or his assistant all the manuscripts they have read that may have merit for possible future publication. He prepares a talk about his "manuscript" to deliver at the weekly editorial meeting, enumerating reasons for its worth, the type of reader to whom it would appeal, and other evaluations he can devise. The editor, whose role is taken by the teacher, can and will probably need to occasionally quiz a reader further on the merits of a book. By this technique many books are exposed to potential readers in the class.

# 95 Why?

Students write a 200-300-word defense of one of the following statements, basing their remarks on a just-read book. Opinions are not enough; they must be reinforced with sound reasoning and logical ideas.

1. This book should be included in a capsule buried today to be dug up in 100 years.
2. This book should be in every English classroom library.
3. This book (if it has been published within the past ten years) should be included in a best books of this decade list.
4. This book should be included in a recommendation list for junior and senior high school readers.
5. This book should be on a list of recommendations for leisure and summertime reading.
6. This book should be required reading for every student who plans to be an English major in college.
7. This book should be read by every thinking American.
8. This book should be read by every adolescent and his parents.
9. This book should win an award.
10. This book should never be spoiled by a teacher requiring a book report.
11. This book should replace ——, which is now required reading in the English course.
12. This book should be removed from the library shelves.
13. This book should be read by every student who hates to read.
14. This book doesn't deserve its popularity.

A lively buzz session can follow these summations, which should make students think, although their opinions may differ considerably from the teacher's as well as their classmates'. If they understand that docile agreement is not required for post-reading communication and reporting, then the objective has been reached.

# 96 Prizewinners All

Many literary awards are given each year in this country and abroad. The Pulitzer Prize Awards are among the most publicized, but a committee investigation of *The World Almanac* and other fact books will reveal much information, not only about the methods of awarding prizes but the titles of books that have won honors. A typed list of the findings can be posted in the library and in the classroom to help students make their reading choices. One or all committee members can summarize the information the group discovered, identifying the sources as well as any available magazine articles located through the *Readers' Guide to Periodical Literature*. Each student chooses a prizewinning title on the list, while the teacher encourages the class to read as many different books as possible. After completing his book, each student writes a 150-200-word paragraph supporting the judges' choice and giving some of the reasons he feels the judges used in reaching their decision. A section of the class, led by a capable student chairman, can discuss some of these points before their peers: What makes these books superior? Are some of them now dated and old-fashioned? Why? How? In general, have many of them remained popular? What is the latest winner? Is there value in seeking out these prizewinners to read?

Each student then summarizes orally the paragraph he wrote on his book, relating his ideas to the discussion and sharing his knowledge of a prizewinner with classmates who may be challenged to expand their personal reading.

# 97 In the Witness Box

Upon completing a general reading assignment, preferably in one category such as the novel or biography, each student prepares three questions that are broad enough to apply to any book in the category, e.g., "What is the chief characteristic of the protagonist of your book?" or "What part does setting play?" The teacher checks the questions, improves them when necessary, and places a successive letter of the alphabet in the upper right-hand corner of each sheet. Each student draws a number and takes his turn in the "witness stand," a chair in the front of the room. The student who composed the questions labeled "A" quizzes student number one about his book, questioner "B" quizzes student number two, and so on. Naturally no one quizzes himself.

Several variations of this activity are possible. For instance, the teacher can be the sole inquisitor or a group of superior students can quiz their classmates one by one.

# 98 For the Reluctant Reader

Teachers often encounter either a hard core of reluctant readers within a class with heterogeneous reading abilities or entire classes of nonreaders. The latter sometimes lack technical ability to read and should receive special assistance from a reading specialist, but often the nonreader simply has no interest in reading because the enormity of the assignments given has discouraged him so that he reacts by not reading anything voluntarily. Any measurable success the teacher has with these students depends upon his ingenuity and creativity to counteract prejudices, laziness, and fear of failure. The following projects are not intended to cover all avenues of approach to the nonreader, but they are practical ideas that will suggest other activities:

1. Students' interest can be piqued by reading aloud a mystery story, stopping before the end and allowing discussion of possible endings. Reading the actual conclusion should spark additional discussion, for all students will not agree with the author's resolution of the plot. This may lead to individual reading of short mystery and detective stories, with the teacher introducing the more capable readers to the classical mystery stories of stature. Depending upon the ability of the group, the teacher can later introduce the mystery drama and the mystery novel. For some classes or individual students an entire semester's reading program can be devoted to mystery stories. If other approaches have failed to develop an interest in reading, then the teacher is justified in experimenting with this approach. The alert teacher is constantly aware of students ready to be moved on into more challenging reading experiences. Relating anecdotes of well-known people who have enjoyed the relaxation of mystery story reading gives status to the pursuit. A clever teacher can introduce some material on the techniques of logical thinking that can be applied as class members discuss individual stories and the paths taken by the plots. The classic mysteries illustrate not only the principles of logic but also the great skill of talented mystery story writers.

A student committee can compose a bibliography, "Mystery

Stories, Great and Not-So-Great," using the school's library resources. Writing a bibliography will give some students composition practice. No reports of any kind should be required for at least a month, then some kind of painless oral reporting could be called for, and finally reports could be written with the students pretending that they are on the staff of mystery story magazines and are responsible for reviews for the magazine's readers.

2. Off-beat subjects such as "Books for Kids Who Like Cars," "Books to Develop Personality," "Books for Self-Improvement," "Books for Mixed-up Teenagers," or similar themes might stimulate reluctant readers. The best way to develop themes for which the library has resources is to make a shelf-by-shelf examination of the books, noting titles that might be of interest. Both the teacher and the students can contribute ideas for themes. After determining the subject, a committee of students, working with the librarian, collects as many books from the shelves as are directly or even vaguely associated with the theme. Reluctant readers are lazy and will respond somewhat if they do not have to hunt for books in the card catalog or on library shelves. The report should be underplayed; the reading is foremost. However, after a reasonable time, some unusual forms of reviewing can be edged into the class activity, such as two or three students arguing diverse views, demonstrations based on self-improvement books, or question-and-answer periods based on the problems of the mixed-up teenagers, with an authority such as the school psychologist, local social workers, or a clergyman as a guest. The home economics teacher, dean of students, or a business teacher could be a guest when the day for discussing books on self-improvement arrives. Never use the word report; emphasize the practicality of the reading and encourage the need to talk about it.

3. Instead of appointing eager readers to a bulletin board committee for the English classroom, assign reluctant readers. They may move with the enthusiasm of snails and need

prodding and advice. During their visit to the library, their conversations with the librarian, and their assignment to explore book possibilities for the display, some members of the committee may see a book that awakens a spark of interest and they may decide to read it. This might be the seed of a developing interest in reading.

4. For some students, reading a book is onerous, and impossible because their attention spans are immaturely short, and teachers can profitably utilize the newspaper to develop reading programs. The short items in the many news departments can train reading ability and develop awareness of the enjoyment to be gained from newspaper reading. After a student learns to lengthen his attention span with this type of reading matter, he can be led into magazine reading, pamphlet reading, and some of them into book reading.

5. The teacher can collect for the classroom some of the pamphlets, brochures, and booklets that the librarian usually keeps in file drawers. Students can be free to read any pamphlets that catch their interest during informal reading sessions, with quiet as the only stipulation. The novelty will be that pamphlets permit almost immediate success in finishing a piece of reading in a relatively short time. Oral talks, preferably informal group discussions, can follow reading sessions.

6. Completely eliminating book reviews as students may have previously known them can be accomplished by organizing the class into editors and reporters for a monthly mimeographed brochure called "Tips for Teenagers." The articles are based upon their supplementary reading. The feature "Car Talk" can be written by the group of boys who own, repair, and worship cars to the exclusion of all other interests. Girls can write articles based on nonfiction reading on dressing well on a budget, cosmetic tricks, manners, and self-improvement. If interest wanes before the end of the semester, shake up the staff by exchanging assignments. Distributing the brochure to teachers and students not in the class encourages the staff to create a quality publication.

7. Vocational students are sometimes reluctant readers, and their primary interests are probably in jobs and money. Use the brochures in the vocational files in the library to create immediacy for their reading. They may never read books, but reading folders of material on airplane mechanics, cosmetology, hospital technicians, auto mechanics, the small business man, or medical secretaries will be realistic and meaningful. For some it will be an easy step to proceed to a related book on the subject. After taking notes, they will be eager to share the discoveries they have made about the requirements of these occupations, the training required, salary range, and opportunities for advancement. Groups within the class can prepare symposiums on related occupations, e.g., the world of business or positions in the electronics field.

 **Books in the Classroom**

Having a variety of books available at all times in a classroom library is a soft-sell way to promote leisure and supplementary reading. Several class librarians can be appointed to set up a simple check-out system and to enforce it. However, building classroom libraries can exhaust the funds of an English department or use up money that might better be invested in records, filmstrips, or other audio-visual supplies. A teacher can suggest that each student pick a paperback from approved book lists supplied by himself or the librarian, purchase it, read it, and prepare a brief talk of two or three minutes on why it is a good choice to donate to the class library. Contributions can be made any time during the year, but the earlier in the term this project is introduced, the more use the donated books will receive. If a student wishes, he can attach a brief summary of his recommendation to the inside front cover to guide others when selecting reading material. Over the course of several years, a sizable library can be built, even though paperbacks do not endure as long as hard-cover books.

A committee of students can work with the teacher in marking each book, using a felt pen, with numbers one through five to indicate the degree of reading difficulty. One can represent very easy, two easy, three average, four difficult, and five very difficult. This guidance will assist students who may begin too difficult books, become discouraged, and stop reading. Every time a student reads a book from the library, he reports to a student clerk who records the number of credits the book was worth. The accumulated record can be reported to the teacher at the end of the marking period for consideration and inclusion in the grade to be issued. The problem of preventing cheating by students desirous of padding their grades can be met by conducting surprise book discussions in which the teacher quizzes students orally on some of the books they have reportedly read. However, the emphasis should be on reading for pleasure, unhampered by required reports of any kind. Including such reading in the mark can be eliminated, but it is a device for encouraging students who can read on a higher level to move up to it under the guise of a reward.

# 100 Expanding by Exchanging

The class pretends that a graduate of the school is currently a Peace Corps member in an African village where he teaches English grammar, composition, and literature to both junior and senior high students in a local school he has helped the villagers to construct. Formerly many of his students attended an English mission school nearby, but political and financial circumstances necessitated its closing. These students, a few of whom plan to enter the university in the faraway capital city, are familiar with the use of the English language. The mission school library, which was donated to the village plus additional books procured by the teacher, is the sole supply of reading material in this isolated community. The Peace Corpsman knows that his students need to expand their horizons and experience not only through reading but by communication with peers beyond their thatched-roofed schoolroom. Therefore, he has requested the cooperation of the English department of his alma mater in an exchange venture of ideas. Supposedly the African students have selected about two dozen titles from their library and have sent a list of the titles and authors to the cooperating class in the American high school. A committee chairman in the American school checks sources for availability. Since this is an imaginary project, the teacher and a student committee can pretend to be the African students and supply the list; current books should be avoided as they would not be in an African library.

Each title is read by two students, who combine their efforts to write an honest, youthful reaction, detailing their commentary to make it informative, thought-provoking, and even controversial if that is appropriate. These literary analyses should strive to emulate journalistic succinctness for they will form the contents of a brochure entitled "Literary Reflections of American Youth," "Literary Exchanges," or "America to Africa, a Journey of Ideas." The booklet's makeup is supervised by an elected editor and staff, with the teacher guiding them in editing the manuscripts; the original writers may rework or revise according to the staff's suggestions. If more realism is desirable, the size of the page can be that of the average paperback. The class will schedule several sessions for discussing general problems as well as the specific weaknesses in the manuscripts. Writing workshops for which students can bring portable typewriters will help to change the classroom atmosphere to that of a busy publisher's offices where the staff is circulating, conferring, and assisting in the revisions and reworkings. The completed brochure is to be sent to the African school where the Peace Corps teacher's students have already read the books. Surely they will find in it much material for discussion, comparison, and enlightenment.

Although this idea has been projected as an imaginary premise, it is very possible that through the proper contacts some kind of actual liaison with a Peace Corps worker and his students can be established. The African students could send handwritten evaluations of the same books. What a fascinating program could be presented for the English Club, the Culture Club, or the book review series the librarian sponsors. Two competent students, working as a dialogue team could alternately present the American points of view in capsule form and then the foreign students' ideas.

If preferred, again through proper channels, a VISTA teacher in some isolated school in the United States or in a ghetto storefront school in a city slum could be contacted for a similar activity. Contact could also be made between a public school in an average community and an Indian mission school of the Southwest, a public school in a ghetto area and a private preparatory school, a large city high school and a rural central school, two schools in divergent geographical areas, a small school and a large school, or other basically different schools where an interchange of ideas can develop a meaningful dialogue and perhaps break down prejudices and misunderstanding.

In some of these situations, economic hardship or limited library facilities may necessitate the more affluent member of the two-school project buying a selection of paperbacks for the project. After they are read, they are sent to the cooperating school where they can be added to the library collection. Money for this project can be raised by sponsoring a secondhand book sale, assessing fines on students late to class or tardy with assignments, or volunteer monetary contributions.

When the written material prepared by one class is received by its counterpart, the ensuing class discussions could be recorded and the tape mailed back to the original class, thus furthering the exchange of viewpoints, information, and areas of agreement. With book reading as the impetus, a creative, mind-stretching experience can be developed for understanding teachers and their average American students who are just waiting to be challenged intellectually.

# Summary of Suggested Uses

## Explanations of Following Charts:

1. If "Written" and/or "Oral" are checked, there are either provisions for a choice or variations requiring either. If "Both" is checked, written and oral activities are required.

2. "General" implies both fiction and nonfiction.

3. If two or three degrees of difficulty are checked, some aspects of the activity are easy, average, or hard, and the teacher can adapt the plan best suited to his students.

4. "Group" implies a small committee of two or as many as fifteen students.

5. "Class" is checked only when some form of active participation by the entire body is required.

6. Although relationship is inferred between the degree of difficulty and the grade level, the teacher can determine if the activity is appropriate for his class by examining the text.

| Activity Number | Form of Report[1] | | | Type of Reading[2] | Degree of Difficulty[3] | | | For Use With | | | Grade Level[6] |
|---|---|---|---|---|---|---|---|---|---|---|---|
| | Written | Oral | Both | | Easy | Average | Hard | Indi-vidual | Group[4] | Class[5] | |
| 1 | X | | | Novel | | X | | X | X | | 7-12 |
| 2 | X | | | General | | X | | X | | | 9-12 |
| 3 | X | X | | Biography | | X | | X | X | | 7-12 |
| 4 | X | | | Shakespeare | | X | | X | X | | 9-12 |
| 5 | | | X | General | | X | | X | X | | 7-12 |
| 6 | | | X | General | | X | | X | X | | 10-12 |
| 7 | | X | | General | X | | | X | | | 7-12 |
| 8 | X | X | | Biography Novel | | X | | X | | | 7-12 |
| 9 | X | X | | Drama | | | X | X | X | | 9-12 |
| 10 | X | X | | Short Story | | | X | X | X | | 7-12 |
| 11 | | | X | General | | X | | | X | | 10-12 |
| 12 | X | | | General | X | | | X | | | 7-12 |
| 13 | X | | | General | | X | X | X | X | | 7-12 |
| 14 | X | | | General | X | X | | X | | | 7-12 |
| 15 | X | | | General | | X | | X | | | 7-12 |
| 16 | | X | | General | X | X | | | X | | 7-12 |
| 17 | X | X | | General | X | X | | X | X | X | 7-12 |

| Activity Number | Form of Report[1] | | | Type of Reading[2] | Degree of Difficulty[3] | | | For Use With | | | Grade Level[6] |
|---|---|---|---|---|---|---|---|---|---|---|---|
| | Written | Oral | Both | | Easy | Average | Hard | Indi-vidual | Group[4] | Class[5] | |
| 18 | X | | | Novel | | X | X | X | X | | 11-12 |
| 19 | X | | | Travel | X | X | | X | | | 7-12 |
| 20 | X | | | General | X | X | X | | X | | 7-12 |
| 21 | X | | | General | X | X | X | | X | | 9-12 |
| 22 | X | | | General | X | X | | X | | | 7-12 |
| 23 | | | X | General | | X | X | | X | | 7-12 |
| 24 | | | X | Biography | X | X | | X | | | 7-12 |
| 25 | | | X | General | | | X | X | | | 11-12 |
| 26 | X | | | General | X | X | | X | | | 7-12 |
| 27 | | | X | General | | X | | X | X | X | 7-12 |
| 28 | X | | | General | X | | | X | | | 7-12 |
| 29 | | X | | General | X | X | | X | | X | 7-12 |
| 30 | | | X | General | | X | X | X | X | | 7-12 |
| 31 | | X | | Nonfiction | X | X | | | X | | 7-12 |
| 32 | X | | | Nonfiction | X | X | | X | | | 7-12 |
| 33 | X | | | General | | X | X | X | | | 9-12 |
| 34 | | | X | General | | X | X | X | | X | 11-12 |
| 35 | X | | | General | X | X | | X | | | 7-12 |

| Activity Number | Form of Report[1] | | | Type of Reading[2] | Degree of Difficulty[3] | | | For Use With | | | Grade Level[6] |
|---|---|---|---|---|---|---|---|---|---|---|---|
| | Written | Oral | Both | | Easy | Average | Hard | Individual | Group[4] | Class[5] | |
| 36 | | | X | General | | X | X | X | X | | 12 |
| 37 | | X | | General | | | X | X | X | | 10-12 |
| 38 | | | X | General | | X | X | X | X | X | 11-12 |
| 39 | | X | | General | X | | | X | | | 7-12 |
| 40 | X | | | General | X | | | X | | | 7-12 |
| 41 | X | | | Magazines | X | | | X | | X | 7-12 |
| 42 | | | X | General | | X | X | X | X | X | 7-12 |
| 43 | | | X | General | | X | | X | X | | 7-12 |
| 44 | | X | | General | | X | X | X | X | X | 7-12 |
| 45 | | X | | Nonfiction | X | X | | X | | | 9-12 |
| 46 | X | X | | Nonfiction | X | X | | X | X | | 10-12 |
| 47 | X | X | | Poetry | X | X | X | X | X | | 7-12 |
| 48 | | X | | Poetry | X | | | X | | | 7-12 |
| 49 | | | X | Poetry | | | X | X | X | X | 12 |
| 50 | X | X | | General | | X | | X | | X | 7-12 |
| 51 | X | | | General | | X | X | X | | | 7-12 |
| 52 | X | X | | Novel | X | X | X | X | X | X | 11-12 |
| 53 | X | | | General | X | X | | X | | | 7-12 |

| Activity Number | Form of Report[1] | | | Type of Reading[2] | Degree of Difficulty[3] | | | For Use With | | | Grade Level[6] |
|---|---|---|---|---|---|---|---|---|---|---|---|
| | Written | Oral | Both | | Easy | Average | Hard | Indi-vidual | Group[4] | Class[5] | |
| 54 | | | X | General | | X | X | X | X | | 11-12 |
| 55 | X | | | Drama | | X | X | X | | | 9-12 |
| 56 | X | | | General | X | X | X | X | | | 9-12 |
| 57 | X | | | General | | | X | X | | X | 11-12 |
| 58 | | | X | General | | X | X | X | X | X | 9-12 |
| 59 | | X | | General | | X | X | X | | | 7-12 |
| 60 | | X | | General | X | X | | X | | | 7-12 |
| 61 | | X | | Biography | | X | X | X | X | | 9-12 |
| 62 | X | | | General | X | X | | X | X | | 7-12 |
| 63 | | | X | Biography | X | X | | X | | X | 7-12 |
| 64 | X | | | Nonfiction | | X | X | X | | X | 9-12 |
| 65 | X | X | | General | | X | X | X | X | X | 11-12 |
| 66 | X | X | | Novel | X | X | | X | X | | 7-12 |
| 67 | | | X | Fiction | | X | | X | X | X | 7-12 |
| 68 | | | X | General | X | X | | X | X | X | 7-12 |
| 69 | | X | | Drama | | X | X | X | X | | 11-12 |
| 70 | | | X | Drama | | X | X | X | | | 10-12 |

| Activity Number | Form of Report[1] | | | Type of Reading[2] | Degree of Difficulty[3] | | | For Use With | | | Grade Level[6] |
|---|---|---|---|---|---|---|---|---|---|---|---|
| | Written | Oral | Both | | Easy | Average | Hard | Indi-vidual | Group[4] | Class[5] | |
| 71 | X | | X | Drama | | X | X | X | X | X | 11-12 |
| 72 | | | X | Fiction | X | X | | | X | | 7-12 |
| 73 | | | X | General | | | X | X | X | | 9-12 |
| 74 | X | X | | General | | X | | X | X | X | 7-12 |
| 75 | X | X | | Short Story Drama | | X | X | X | | | 7-12 |
| 76 | | X | | Poetry, Drama, Biography | X | X | | X | | | 7-12 |
| 77 | | | X | Novel | | X | X | X | X | | 11-12 |
| 78 | X | X | | Nonfiction | X | X | | X | | | 9-12 |
| 79 | | | X | General | | X | | X | X | X | 7-12 |
| 80 | X | X | | General | | X | X | X | X | X | 7-12 |
| 81 | | | X | General | | X | X | X | X | X | 7-12 |
| 82 | | | X | General | X | | | X | | X | 7-12 |
| 83 | | X | | General | | X | | X | | | 7-12 |
| 84 | | | X | General | | | X | X | | X | 11-12 |
| 85 | X | X | | Travel | | X | | X | | X | 7-12 |

| Activity Number | Form of Report[1] | | | Type of Reading[2] | Degree of Difficulty[3] | | | For Use With | | | Grade Level[6] |
|---|---|---|---|---|---|---|---|---|---|---|---|
| | Written | Oral | Both | | Easy | Average | Hard | Indi-vidual | Group[4] | Class[5] | |
| 86 | X | X | | Novel | | X | | X | X | X | 7-12 |
| 87 | X | | | General | | X | X | X | X | | 9-12 |
| 88 | | X | | General | X | X | | X | X | | 7-12 |
| 89 | X | | | General | | X | X | X | | | 9-12 |
| 90 | X | X | | General | | X | | X | | X | 7-12 |
| 91 | X | | | General | X | X | | X | | | 7-12 |
| 92 | | | X | General | | X | X | X | X | | 9-12 |
| 93 | | X | | General | | X | X | X | X | | 11-12 |
| 94 | | X | | General | | X | | X | | | 7-12 |
| 95 | | | X | General | X | X | | X | | | 7-12 |
| 96 | | | X | General | X | X | | X | X | X | 11-12 |
| 97 | | | X | General | X | X | | X | | X | 7-12 |
| 98 | | | X | General | X | X | | X | X | X | 7-12 |
| 99 | | | X | General | | X | | X | X | | 7-12 |
| 100 | | | X | General | | X | X | X | X | X | 7-12 |

# Selected Sources for Teachers and/or Students

## Reading Improvement and Enrichment

Adler, Mortimer J. *Great Ideas from Great Books.* New York: Washington Square, 1961.

Problems and conditions of life as treated by the great books of the ages. Useful to students and teachers for developing reading programs based on such subjects as war and peace, political developments, the role of women in society, and dozens of others. Indicates how students can get their own "great ideas" from reading.

————. *How to Read a Book.* New York: Simon and Schuster, 1956.

Traces the relationship of reading to learning and thinking. Hints and techniques for reading all types of material, the nature of critical reading, advice on improving reading ability, and applying reading to life's problems. List of the world's best books for a lifetime reading program. The recognized classic of its type in the field.

Allen, Walter. *The English Novel.* New York: Dutton, 1954.

Recognized authority explains how to distinguish between good and bad literature. Discusses many books in detail. Combines historical and critical approaches.

————. *The Modern Novel in Britain and the United States.* New York: Dutton, 1964.

Brilliant criticism on most of the important novels since World War I, discussing the essence of each with intellectual understanding and biting humor. Broad areas covered, but treatment is detailed and will increase appreciation of all reading of this genre.

Bamman, Henry A., and others. *Reading Instruction in the Secondary Schools.* New York: McKay, 1961.

Problems of teaching reading in high school and methods of overcoming them. Especially helpful for new teachers.

Beach, Joseph W. *English Literature of the 19th and Early 20th Centuries, 1798 to the First World War,* vol. IV of *A History of English Literature.* New York: Crowell-Collier, 1962.

Spans a period from Wordsworth to Yeats and his contemporaries, with evaluations of Victorian essayists, novelists, and poets, the influences of the Industrial Revolution, and the effects of the philosophies of Darwin, Marx, and Freud on literary thought. Material will enrich literature-in-depth studies for superior students; provides pleasant, palatable reference source for students' research.

Bentley, Eric. *In Search of Theater.* New York: Random, 1954.

A critic deals with playwrights, actors, producers, other critics, and audiences in Europe and the United States for the period spanning World War II to 1954.

Carlsen, G. Robert. *Books and the Teenage Reader.* New York: Bantam, 1967.

An indispensable book for teachers, librarians, and parents. Nine bibliographies, most of them annotated. Suggests reading programs to awaken student enthusiasm and to improve communication between the generations.

Center, Stella. *Art of Book Reading.* New York: Scribner, 1952.

Guide to aid the intelligent reader to add variety to his reading, improve his comprehension, and enjoy the experience more fully. Considers reading techniques and their application, the role of the classics, and the implications of vocational success through effective reading.

Drew, Elizabeth. *Poetry: A Modern Guide to Its Understanding and Enjoyment.* New York: Dell, 1959.

Discusses the techniques of the poet: language, symbolism, rhythms, and others; second part is devoted to the themes of poetry: love, religion, humanism, and others. A profusion of examples of English and American poetry from the 16th through the 20th century.

Eisinger, Chester. *Fiction of the Forties.* Chicago: U. of Chicago, 1963.

Examines the elements of the century that influenced the novelists, liberally illustrated with references to specific works. Pleasant to read, understandable, and authoritative.

Fader, Daniel M., and McNeil, Elton B. *Hooked on Books: Program and Proof.* New York: Berkley, 1968.

Dramatic reading program that succeeded in getting "losers" to read, read, read. Based on theories of saturation and diffusion, combined with daily written reactions to reading to promote fluency and communication. 1,000 suggested paperbacks.

Goddard, Harold. *The Meaning of Shakespeare.* Chicago: U. of Chicago, 1951.

Informative, personal viewpoints of an authority who treats characterization and plots enlighteningly and enthusiastically; strong on character interpretation.

Gohdes, Clarence. *Literature and Theater of the States and Regions of the U.S.A.* Durham: Duke U., 1967.

Valuable reference book of 6,000 entries, giving information about the literature about each state and region. Teachers of American literature will welcome its contributions to supplementary and class reading programs on cultural characteristics and developments on regional levels.

Granville-Barker, H., and Harrison, G. B. *A Companion to Shakespeare Studies.* Garden City: Doubleday, 1960.

Fifteen essays on producers, actors, and spectators of the plays; complete guide to the playwright and his works. Considers other playwrights of the time and surveys dramatic criticism of Shakespeare from Dryden to the present. Indispensable to any study or reading of the plays.

Gross, Seymour L., and Hardy, John E. *Images of the Negro in American Literature.* Chicago: U. of Chicago, 1966.

Deals with traditions and conventions in the literary depiction of the Negro by individual authors, both Negro and white, somewhat in an historical progression.

Grozier, Edwin A. *Plot Outlines of 101 Best Novels.* New York: Barnes and Noble, 1962.

Generous three-to-five-page condensations based on novels usually found on high school lists, especially those for the college-bound.

Harris, Albert J. *How to Increase Reading Ability: A Guide to Developmental and Remedial Methods,* 4th ed. New York: McKay, 1961.

Treats factors increasing readiness, problems of individual and group reading, causes of reading disabilities, improvements possible in technical ability, and a bibliography of workbooks, materials, and books for reading improvement.

Highet, Gilbert. *People, Places, and Books*. New York: Oxford, 1953.
Radio talks, printed as an essay collection, on the art of writing, the appreciation of the various genres of literature, and fascinating behind-the-stories stories, with some evaluations and considerations of the best sellers up to 1953. Also helpful as examples of how to make oral book talks entertaining and informative.

Hove, John, *Meeting Censorship in the Schools*. Champaign: NCTE.
Examples and case studies of objections made by individuals to certain books sometimes included in English classrooms and libraries. Successful and unsuccessful experiences in meeting the challenges of censorship.

Jennings, Frank G. *This Is Reading*. New York: Dell, 1965.
A teacher of communication-English and an editor presents an inclusive treatment of reading in its historical, sociological, and educational settings. Written with enthusiasm and know-how with an abundance of examples and suggestions.

Kendall, Paul M. *Art of Biography*. New York: Norton, 1965.
A noted author and critic explores the processes and problems of writing about people. Future biography reading will be more worthwhile and enjoyable because of this behind-the-scenes disclosure.

Krutch, Joseph Wood. *Modernism in Modern Drama: A Definition and an Estimate*. Ithaca, N.Y.: Cornell U., 1953.
Essays, which define the usually vague term "modernism" in beliefs, attitudes, and judgments. Examines the general thesis from a moral and literary viewpoint, expanding it with examples and application to Ibsen, Shaw, and other "moderns."

Leary, Lewis. *The Teacher and American Literature*. Champaign: NCTE, 1965.
Twenty-four papers on all phases of the subject by experts in all the literary forms. Reveals recent developments and new techniques and philosophies.

Lewis, Norman. *How to Become a Better Reader*. New York: Macfadden, 1964.
Practical and theoretical assistance for the reader who wishes to obtain more enjoyment from reading.

MacCampbell, Donald. *Reading for Enjoyment*. New York: Macfadden, 1964.
Straightforward methods of how to read, what to read, and how to retain what is read.

Pilgrim, Geneva H., and McAllister, Marion K. *Books, Young People, and Reading Guidance*, 2nd ed. New York: Harper, 1968.

Needs of youth, proposed reading guidance programs to meet those needs, and recommended book lists.

Priestley, John B. *Literature and Western Man*. New York: Harper and Row, 1960.

Mind-expanding book by experienced writer on thesis that man can be understood through his literature. Written for readers, not scholars, who want to learn what is significant in the world of writers and their works.

Pritchett, Victor S. *The Living Novel and Later Appreciations*. New York: Random, 1947.

Critical essays on major writers from Conrad to William Golden with detours for minor writers. Comprehendible study in an easy style that can make future novel reading more meaningful.

Rosenheim, Edward W., Jr. *What Happens in Literature: A Guide to Poetry, Drama, and Fiction*. Chicago: U. of Chicago, 1960.

Provides information, raises questions, and offers suggestions to increase students' enjoyment of literature. Contents include: reading lyric poems, narrative fiction, dramatic literature, poems as historical fact, and an analysis of how best to read and consider all these areas.

Stauffer, Donald. *The Nature of Poetry*. New York: Norton, 1962.

Defines poetry by viewing it from many angles. Explains exactness, intensity, significance, correctness, complexity, rhythm, and formality for the layman or serious student.

Stefferud, Alfred. *Wonderful World of Books*. New York: New American Library, 1952.

Chapters on books as friends, the pleasures of reading, the art of reading more effectively, and advice on choosing and using a book both as a reader and as a teacher.

Taaffe, James G. *Students' Guide to Literary Terms*. New York: World, 1967.

Explains all the usual and some of the unusual terminology applicable to literature, its elements, and its criticism. Enables teachers and students to communicate in oral and written media with intelligent understanding. A must for every English classroom and teacher's library.

Thompson, Denys. *Reading and Discrimination*. New York: Hillary, 1965.

175

Formation of taste by readers and the development of intelligent standards of values, particularly through repeated writing of criticism, is the purpose of this excellent book for secondary students. Teaches directly the skills of criticizing with sample passages for students to criticize and then compare with author's criticism. Suggested reading list.

Walch, J. Weston, ed. *Successful Devices in Teaching Literature.* Portland, Me.: J. Weston Walch, 1960.

Plans for teaching about literature and authors; specific plans for developing extensive supplementary reading.

Wright, Austin McGiffert. *The American Short Story in the Twenties.* Chicago: U. of Chicago, 1961.

More than 15 categories are considered, such as moral principles, acceptance of adversity, commitment to others, and failure of love. Analytical guide to the era.

## LITERARY CRITICISM

Some of the lack of success with book reports in the junior and senior high school classes is directly due to lack of acquaintance with the real nature of literary criticism. Too often the teacher himself is vague in his own concepts, or he assumes that students automatically react constructively to their in-class and supplementary reading. Many experts have defined criteria for judging literary values, both by examining individual literary works or separate genres. These suggestions may assist both teachers and students to sharpen their critical instincts and build bases of critical methods and approaches.

Adelman, Irving, and Dworkin, Rita. *Modern Drama: A Checklist of Critical Literature on 20th Century Plays.* Metuchen, N.J.: Scarecrow, 1967.

Selective survey and guide to the critical literature of 20th century English and foreign language drama. Uses the resources of 800 books to apply to 1,000 plays. Valuable reference.

Barnet, Sylvan, and others. *Study of Literature: A Handbook of Critical Essays and Terms.* Boston: Little Brown, 1960.

Important essays on principles of analyzing literature and some of the problems of literary study. Considers all the genres of literature from Greek to modern English and American. Valuable dictionary of literary terms, defined and illustrated.

Berry, Thomas Elliot. *The Biographer's Craft.* New York: Odyssey, 1967.

Describes biography through the biographer's eyes, mind, and understanding and explains the elements of the craft itself with biographical selections for analysis and discussion based on 12 searching questions.

Blackmur, Richard P. *Form and Value in Poetry.* Garden City, N.Y.: Doubleday, 1957.

Essays that examine poetry in all aspects from linguistic techniques to intellectual and emotional forms. Theories defined are directly applied to Yeats, Hardy, Pound, and other giants. Includes Tennyson's famous essay "A Critic's Job of Work."

Bowen, Catherine D. *Biography: The Craft and the Calling.* Boston: Little Brown, 1969.

A distinguished biographer explores the hows and whys of writing biography with many examples and anecdotes and candid analyses of her own and others' works. Will sharpen biography appreciation and aid in criticism.

Cole, Toby. *Playwrights on Playwriting.* New York: Hill and Wang, 1960.

Essays by Ionesco, Miller, Osborne, Brecht, Sartre, and others, which can be used to develop standards of criteria for criticism as suggested by writers themselves.

*Critical Biographies of English Authors* (Twayne series) and *Critical Biographies of English Authors* (Twayne Second series). Champaign: NCTE.

Compact, critical, and analytical studies of the life and works of important authors; bibliographies of works of each.

Clurman, Harold. *Lies Like Truth.* New York: Grove, 1958.

Collection of theatrical reviews written primarily for magazines. Interesting for their outspoken reactions to plays, playhouses, and performers and will provide students with models to imitate in dramatic criticism.

Daiches, David. *Critical Approaches to Literature.* New York: Prentice Hall, 1965.

A comprehensive study of the methods, functions, and values of criticism from its early beginning to the present. Extremely helpful to teachers and pre-college students.

————. *A Study of Literature for Readers and Critics.* New York: Norton, 1964.

An expert explores the functions and purposes of imaginative literature with abundant illustrations of the various theses and references from the classics to the contemporary.

Deutsch, Babette. *Poetry in Our Time: Critical Survey of Poetry in the English Speaking World 1900-1960*, rev. ed. Garden City, N.Y.: Doubleday, 1963.

Deals with trends, forms, and content of poetry in general and some poems in particular to show that poetry grows out of life, and how in return, it nourishes life. Author's purpose is to make poetry understandable to the intelligent reader and to examine the growth of modern poetry.

Dickinson, Leon. *A Guide to Literary Study*. New York: Holt, Rinehart and Winston, 1967.

A general inquiry into the role of criticism for all literature, followed by individual treatment of all the genres as to nature and elements. Handy paperback guide all students should have.

*Discussion of Literature* (D. C. Heath's series). Champaign: NCTE.

Each volume is an anthology of critical comment edited by a specialist on a type of literature, such as *Poetry: Rhythm and Sound,* a specific work of literature, such as *Canterbury Tales,* or an author, such as Jane Austen. Essays in each book are arranged chronologically to give students a balanced view of the development of critical opinion.

Fergusson, Francis. *The Idea of A Theater: The Art of Drama in Changing Perspective*. Garden City, N.Y.: Doubleday, 1953.

Critical study of ten classic plays from Sophocles to T. S. Eliot, not from an historical vantage but from the basic concepts of drama with emphases on realism, techniques, character development, and the dramatist's skills. Excellent examples of literary analyses for students seeking background and direction.

Jarrell, Randall. *Poetry and the Age*. New York: Random, 1953.

Describes both intellectual and practical criticism with penetrating insights and evaluations of some of the best and a few of the worst American poets. Examines the nature of modern poetry and the age that created it.

Kerr, Walter. *Tragedy and Comedy*. New York: Simon and Schuster, 1967.

Traces drama from ancient times to today in a scholarly but enjoyable style.

Lawson, John H. *Theory and Techniques of Playwriting*. New York: Hill and Wang, 1960.

Standard book in the field on the history of dramatic thought, the theater today, dramatic structure, and dramatic composition. Gives students insights to aid his appreciation of and critical attitudes to this complex art form.

McDonald, Daniel. *Controversy: Logic in Writing and Reading*. San Francisco: Chandler, 1967.

Text explains briefly six elements of logical thinking and provides six large subjects such as the Negro, censorship, and others, each with seven literary pieces on the subject followed by questions for discussing it and some suggested follow-up essay subjects. Splendid to use in teaching students to read and react to argument critically.

Richards, Ivor A. *Principles of Literary Criticism*. New York: Harcourt, Brace and World, 1968.

Analyzes all the criteria, psychological, emotional, and technical, of the skill and art of literary criticism.

Stewart, Joyce S., and Burkett, Eva M. *Introducing Reading in Literary Criticism*. Menlo Park, Cal.: Addison Wiley, 1968.

Essays to aid students to understand their reading, appreciate writing techniques, and explore elements of style, humor, satire, and criticism. Includes analyses of all the genres of literature and an explanation of the vocabulary useful and imperative for literary criticism. Intended for secondary students.

Styan, J. L. *The Elements of Drama*. London, New York: Cambridge U., 1967.

This introduction to drama discusses the various elements of the literary form.

*Teaching World Literature in the High School* (38603). Champaign: NCTE, 1968.

Emphasizes the necessity for including world literature in formal literary study and in leisure reading programs. Sample suggested programs.

Zitner, Sheldon P., and others. *Preface to Literary Analysis*. Chicago: Scott, Foresman, 1964.

Considers literature and the humanities, the language of poetry, the nature of narrative, style in writing, and the techniques of the drama. Practical listings of vocabulary for criticism and many examples of written evaluations and interpretations. Excellent for secondary schools.

De Vitis, A. A. *Words in Context: A Vocabulary Builder*, 2nd ed. New York: Appleton-Century-Crofts, 1968.

Using excerpts of literature, the 20 sections are designed to build vocabulary on the basis of reading and usage. The essays and excerpts have appeal for students of diverse interests and backgrounds. Proceeds from less difficult to difficult; includes some scientific and technical vocabulary.

Drewry, John E. *Writing Book Reviews*. Boston: The Writer, 1966.

Although the advice is intended for professional and free-lance writers who want to review books, it has great value for students in the step-by-step help for beginners on how to evaluate books in many fields and how to review for newspapers and magazines. Lists literary prizes and awards.

Flesch, Rudolf. *How to Write, Speak, and Think More Effectively*. New York: Harper and Row, 1960.

This minor classic, often reprinted, is a complete step-by-step course in communication that gives a systematic program for self-improvement. Many exercises and methods.

Howard, Daniel. *Writing About Reading: A Practical Rhetoric and a Writer's Handbook*. Boston: Little Brown, 1966.

Helps students to respond to the written word and express that response in good prose and exposes the student to a wide range of expository and literary writing. Part I is an inquiry into analytical reading and writing; Part II is a useful, compact writer's handbook.

Karner, Edwin J., and Cordell, C. *Successful School Publications*. Portland, Me.: J. Weston Walch, 1959.

Complete guidance for creating school or classroom newspapers and magazines. Generously illustrated. Useful for book reports that require a journalistic format.

Kinnick, Jo B., ed. *The School Literary Magazine* (31806). Champaign: NCTE, 1966.

Ideas for stimulating student writing and suggestions for a school or classroom literary magazine; useful to the literature teacher requiring a literary magazine format book report.

Laird, Charlton, and others. *Guide for Objective Writing*. Boston: Ginn, 1967.

For students in grades 11 and 12 doing research papers and needing to handle facts and opinions. Excellent examples of generalization, qualification, assumption, bias, and connotation.

Perlmutter, Jerome H. *Practical Guide to Effective Writing.* New York: Dell, 1965.

Directed at anyone, adult or student, who seeks effective communication through the written word. Convenient, useful book on good expository writing through correct preparation, writing, and revision. Extremely apropos to the writing of book reviews.

Roer, Berniece. *How to Write Articles.* St. Louis: Bethany, 1963.

Considers conceiving ideas, format, types of articles, rewriting, and marketing. Compact, direct, and understandable.

*Teachers' Guide for High School Journalism* (48503). Champaign: NCTE, 1965.

All phases of producing high school newspapers and magazines; useful for English teachers whose students use the journalistic media suggested in some of these novel ways with book reports.

*Theories of Style and Their Implication for the Teaching of Composition and Other Essays* (32805). Champaign: NCTE, 1965.

The difficult and often obscure concept of style in writing is examined in all its aspects by many authorities. Teachers will find the many opinions helpful.

Thomas, Ednah S. *Evaluating Student Themes.* Madison: U. of Wisconsin, 1960.

Compares unsatisfactory quality, middle quality, and superior quality themes with specific guidance for the teacher on how to make corrections meaningful for the students.

## ORAL COMMUNICATION

Flesch, Rudolf. *The Art of Clear Thinking.* New York: Harper, 1951.

Simplified explanation of how to present ideas and develop constructive argument. Although intended for general application, the theories apply directly to presenting both written and oral criticism of literature. Can be easily comprehended by average and high-ability students.

Garland, Jasper V. *Discussion Methods,* 3rd ed. New York: Wilson, 1951.

Requirements for discussion, citing methods and examples for individual speakers, leaders, or participants in informal discussions or formal debates, forums, symposia, or radio discourses. Excellent for teachers and students who want to improve the quality of oral approaches to the book report.

Green, J. H. C. *Speak to Me*. New York: Odyssey, 1962.

A lecturer and speech teacher provides psychological and practical help for the nervous, amateur speaker in building confidence, delivery, audience relationships, speech preparation, contents, and the final performance.

Holm, James W. *Successful Discussion and Debate*. Portland, Me.: J. Weston Walch, 1960.

The hows and whys of debate plus discussion leadership and participation techniques explained in brief, direct, and useful form by a debate professor.

Larson, Orvin. *When It's Your Turn to Speak*. New York: Harper, 1962.

Functional, effective procedures and workable suggestions and hints for all-occasion speaking situations.

Moffett, James. *Drama: What Is Happening* (17751). Champaign: NCTE, 1967.

Shows how drama and speech are vehicles for developing ideas and communication.

Oppenheimer, Evelyn. *Book Reviewing for an Audience: A Practical Guide for Lecturers and Broadcasters*. Philadelphia: Chilton, 1962.

Describes the selection and preparation of materials and the important aspects of presentation; includes sample reviews that reveal clever approaches and techniques.

Quimby, Brooks. *So You Want to Discuss and Debate*. Portland, Me.: J. Weston Walch, 1959.

Written for beginning debaters. Considers specifically the organization, preparation, and presentation of classroom and school debates as well as the best techniques of group discussion. Practical for junior and senior high school.

## AUDIO-VISUAL AIDS

The following items were selected from the hundreds of audio-visual materials pertinent to many of the book reporting activities described in this volume; there are many, many more that would be equally useful. Most film and filmstrip producers, record companies, and educational publishers with audio-visual departments will send descriptive catalogs on request, and listings may also be obtained from periodicals and professional organizations specializing in audio-visual media.

Allison, Mary L., ed. *New Educational Materials*. New York: Citation, 1967 and 1968.

Each volume contains over 600 evaluations of current instructional aids, including audio-visual tools. Based on classroom tryouts by experienced teachers, librarians, and curriculum specialists. Invaluable resource book for all teachers.

Coltharp, Joe. *Production of 2" x 2" Slides for School Use*. Austin: Visual Instruction Bureau, U. of Texas, 1967.

Simple, well-illustrated procedures for teacher- or student-created slides.

*Constructing Reports* (61006) (6FS). Champaign: NCTE.

Series showing how to collect facts, select a theme, and build reports.

*Forms of Poetry* (2 12" 33⅓ records). Champaign: NCTE.

Illustrations of the classic forms of poetry and a section on metrics.

*Fundamentals of Writing* (6 color FS, student workpads, teaching guides). Pleasantville, N.Y.: Educational Audio Visual.

Choosing the topic and getting the facts, building the framework, linking the parts to make the whole, style, revising, and structure are the topics covered.

Horn, George F. *Bulletin Boards*. New York: Chapman-Reinhold, 1962.

Profusely illustrated. Explains the processes and techniques of using bulletin boards as effective teaching tools.

Hornick, Joanne. *Creative Bulletin Boards for Junior High School*. New York: Citation, 1968.

Suggests and illustrates the use of humor, color, and design to enliven bulletin boards in English and language arts classes.

*How to Read Literature* (6 FS). Champaign: NCTE.

History, novel, one-act play, historical novel, and short story.

Lewis, Shari. *Making Easy Puppets*. New York: Dutton, 1967.

Wide range of puppet-making ideas with illustrations. Chapters on history of puppets, stage making, puppet costumes, origami puppets, etc.

*Literary Maps*. Champaign: NCTE.

Individual states, sections of and entire United States, and some sections of the world, past and present.

*The Nature of Poetry* (1 12" 33⅓ record). Champaign: NCTE.

Dr. Frank Baxter lectures on the essence of poetry.

*Organizing Your Writing* (8 color FSs). Encyclopaedia Britannica Films.

Clarifies the organizational patterns of expository writing to aid high school students in achieving more logical organization in the type of writing required for critical reading and other reports.

Rufswold, Margaret, and Guss, Carolyn. *Guides to Newer Educational Media: Films, Filmstrips, Phono-records, Slides, Radio and TV,* 2nd ed. Chicago: American Library Association, 1967.

Includes a section on audio-visual aids. Describes available catalogs, lists journals and periodicals that give advice and aid in using audio-visual materials, and covers the widening area of their application.

Schreiber, Morris. *An Annotated List of Recordings in the Language Arts.* Champaign: NCTE, 1964.

Listed by subject matter and class placement; distributors and addresses, prices.

Smith, Richard E. *The Overhead System, Implementation and Utilization.* Austin: Visual Instruction Bureau, U. of Texas, 1968.

Nontechnical handbook for the classroom teacher on the role of the overhead projector in teaching.

*Sound of World Poetry* (1 LP and script). Folkways/Scholastic.

Combines educational effectiveness with musical beauty of poetry in 15 languages. Script contains text of poetry in the original language with interlinear translations to enable the listener to hear the tonal qualities while following the English meanings.

*Today's Poets: Their Poems—Their Voices,* vol. I and II; others in preparation. (2 12″ LPs with pamphlet containing text of poems and statements of the poets about their poetry.) Folkways/Scholastic.

Each record has four of the best modern poets. The eye and ear combination of poetry appreciation is effective. Suitable for grades 9 through 12. Bibliographies of poets' work included.

*Understanding and Appreciation of the Novel* (1 12″ LP). Folkways/Scholastic.

Instructive and highly entertaining presentation of the history and criticism of the novel: techniques, literary types, and discussion of famous novels. Excellent example for students of how to criticize literature. *Understanding and Appreciation of Poetry* (1 12″ LP) defines rhythms, language, and structure with examples by many voices, and *Understanding and Appreciation of the Short Story* (1 12″ LP) discusses the art of the short story, mood, setting, action, characterization, important writers and themes, questions and answers, roots, and comparisons with other literary types.

*Vocabulary Improvement Series* (5 12" 33⅓ records, study guide and test sheets). Champaign: NCTE.

Script written by Dr. Bergen Evans, language expert. Each record features 100 selected words found in newspapers, magazines, and books, words often recognized but not understood. Particularly good study to aid students in written and oral book reviews.

## WRITING INCENTIVES

Teachers can raise the levels of student interest by creating an atmosphere for learning based on practical incentives that give immediacy and authenticity to writing assignments. For instance, national, regional, and local writing contests provide materialistic and status inducements and give creative students opportunities to have their talents discovered.

*Scholastic Creative Writing Awards*, 50 West 44th St., New York, N.Y. 10036.

A national contest for students in grades 7 through 12 attending schools in the United States, its territories, Canada, or a United States school abroad has been recognized throughout its 45-year history as a major event for student writing. The Senior Division accepts entries from students in grades 10, 11, and 12 in these classifications: short story, short-short story, poetry, informal article, formal article, dramatic script, and critical review. The Junior Division for grades 7, 8, and 9 has entry classifications in: short story, poetry, and articles. Incentives are cash prizes for top winners and honorable mentions and certificates of merit for runners-up, with two awards for outstanding ability winners. Some of the winning entries are published in Scholastic's student magazines, and opportunities for further publication are possible. Sponsored jointly with Royal Portable Typewriter, the contest has often proved a catalyst for many teenage writers who went on to become successful novelists, poets, journalists, editors, and dramatists. The Senior Division offers the possibility for entry in the formal article category of a personal commentary on a work of literature of the kind suggested in some of the activities that concentrate on formal critiques or literary analyses. The rules booklet for this contest, which has a due date for entries in the early spring, is available on request between October and February.

For information about other writing contests, contact:

*The Student Writer,* 2651 North Federal Highway, Fort Lauderdale, Florida 33300.

*Seventeen,* 320 Park Avenue, New York, N.Y. 10022.

*The Atlantic,* 8 Arlington St., Boston, Mass. 02116.

*Harper's Magazine,* 2 Park Avenue, New York, N.Y. 10016.

*Partnership Program,* Peace Corps, Washington, D.C.

A cultural exchange program in which students in an American school adopt a specific school or community of a Peace Corps worker for the creation of understanding of peoples and cultures. Suggestions for types of practical activities are contained in the *How to Do It Kit* available on request. A possibility that fits the requirements of the suggested exchanges is specifically detailed in Activity 100, but many other activities could lead to a similar exchange.

## BIBLIOGRAPHIES AND BIBLIOGRAPHICAL AIDS

In addition to the specific titles suggested below, specialized bibliographies, reading lists, and catalogs may be obtained from many sources:

State departments of education and their individual departments, i.e., Bureau of Guidance, New York State Department of Education.

Metropolitan and county public libraries.

Federal and state government agencies, i.e., Office of Education, Department of Health, Education and Welfare, Washington, D.C.

Publishing companies, i.e., R. R. Bowker Company; *New York Times,* Book and Educational Division.

National and state professional associations, i.e., American Library Association; National Council of Teachers of English; National Education Association.

Service clubs and societies, i.e., Jaycees Good Reading for Youth Program, Pilgrim Book Society, Akron, Ohio.

Child-centered and child-study organizations, i.e., Association for Childhood Education International.

National religious organizations, i.e., National Conference of Christians and Jews.

Special-interest groups such as conservation, civil rights, or good government, i.e., B'nai B'rith; American Civil Liberties Union.

Alm, R. S. *Books for You.* New York: Simon and Schuster, 1964.

Reading list for grades 9 through 12 to assist students to build a lifetime habit of reading for pleasure. Individual and group programs well illustrated and annotated.

Benét, William Rose. *The Readers' Encyclopedia.* New York: Crowell, 1965.

Literature, art, mythology, music, and biographical data.

Boylan, Lucille. *A Catalogue of Paperbacks for Grades 7-12.* Metuchen, N.J.: Scarecrow, 1963.

1,000 annotated titles.

*Canadian Books for Schools* (42457). Champaign: NCTE, 1968.

An annotated list giving grade level and subject area relevance for each title.

Courtney, Winifred F. *The Reader's Advisor: A Guide to the Best in Literature,* vol. I. New York: Bowker, 1969.

Every genre of literature from antiquity to the present with historical facts, criticisms, and book lists with pertinent data on 2,500 works. Combines the best of a bibliography with a source book of facts, historical and critical.

―――. *The Readers' Advisor: The Layman's Guide to the Best in Print,* vol. II. New York: Bowker, available in late 1969.

Lists books on biography, the Bible, world religions, philosophy, the sciences, the lively arts, travel, folklore, and history. Includes biographies of authors, anecdotes about books and authors, and quotations from critics.

Crosly, Muriel. *Reading Ladders for Human Relations.* Washington: American Council on Education, 1963.

Reading programs in human relations for elementary, secondary, and adult readers with annotated bibliographies.

Dodds, Barbara. *Negro Literature for High School Students.* Champaign: NCTE, 1968.

Reviews 150 books and suggests unit and lesson plans. Includes Detroit curriculum supplement on Negro literature for ninth-grade study.

Eakin, Mary K. *Good Books for Children.* Chicago: U. of Chicago, 1966.

1,300 annotated suggestions for all age groups for books 1950-1965.

Emery, Raymond C., and Houshower, Margaret. *High Interest, Easy Reading for Junior and Senior High School Reluctant Readers* (43009). Champaign: NCTE, 1965.

Reading suggestions based on a reading inventory; reading ability and interest levels indicated.

Evertts, Eldonna L. *Dimensions of Dialect* (24903). Champaign: NCTE.

Introductory material of importance to teachers for the implications of dialect differences in student groups. Excellent accompanying bibliography for bilingual children and those learning English as a second language.

Haebich, Kathryn A. *Vocations in Biography and Fiction.* Chicago: American Library Association, 1962.

Particularly useful for reluctant readers. 1,070 titles annotated.

Keating, Charlotte M. *Building Bridges of Understanding.* Tucson: Palo Verde Pub., 1967.

Unusual listing of books for children from non-English-speaking homes from elementary through high school. Specific suggestions for Negro, American Indian, Spanish-speaking, Chinese-American, Japanese-American, Hawaiian, Jewish, and other minority groups. Reading aimed at self-understanding as well as appreciation of other people and their cultures.

*Kliatt Paperback Guide to Current Paperbacks.* Newton, Mass., 6 Crocker Circle W.: Kliatt.

A new selected paperback guide in a loose-leaf format with monthly additions. Long, detailed annotations include subject headings, reading ability, and age.

Mersand, Joseph, and others. *Guide to Play Selection,* 2nd ed. Champaign: NCTE, 1958.

430 full-length and 294 one-act plays. Includes brief discussions of each period of drama from the Greek to 1958.

O'Neal, Robert. *Teachers' Guide to World Literature for the High School* (38408). Champaign: NCTE, 1966.

Thematic arrangement of 200 books with detailed annotations; includes non-western selections in translation.

*Paperback Goes to School.* New York: Bureau of Independent Publishers and Distributors.

Annual free list of paperback titles useful and available for classroom and supplementary reading programs.

*A Reading List of High Interest-Low Vocabulary Books for Enrichment in Various Areas of the Curriculum.* Storrs: Reading Study Center, U. of Conn., 1965.

Of particular value in promoting some of the activities of this book that require cooperation with other school departments such as history, music, and art. Keyed to the needs of the less able reader.

*Senior Book List: Current Books.* Boston: National Association of Independent Schools, pub. annually.

A feature of this comprehensive listing is the list of the ten best adult books of the year recommended for the pre-college reader.

Sorghum, T. *Bibliography of World Literature 1930-1963.* Metuchen, N.J.: Scarecrow, 1963.

Useful in planning a world literature study or a historical or comparative approach to literary trends on a worldwide basis.

Spiegler, Charles G. *100 Tested Books for Retarded Readers.* Chicago: Rand McNally, 1964.

Carefully considered listing of books that have proved successful with students hampered by technical difficulties in reading, not to be confused with the reluctant reader.

Strang, Ruth, and others. *Gateways to Readable Books,* 4th ed. New York: Wilson, 1966.

Books for students with reading abilities below that expected for the average high school student; annotations indicate the degree of difficulty. More than 1,000 entries.

*A Subject List of Historical Fiction for Young Adult Reading.* Berkley, Cal.: College Library Association.

Particularly useful annotated suggestions.

Sullivan, Helen B., and Tolman, L. E. *High Interest-Low Vocabulary Reading Material.* Boston: Boston U. School of Ed., 1964.

Books to solve some of the problems of reading when working with the mildly or seriously disadvantaged child.

Weber, J. Sherwood, and others. *Good Reading.* New York: Bowker, 1960.

Advice on how to choose books to meet specific needs, interests, and reading problems of individual students. Book lists for many subject fields and for all the literary genres.

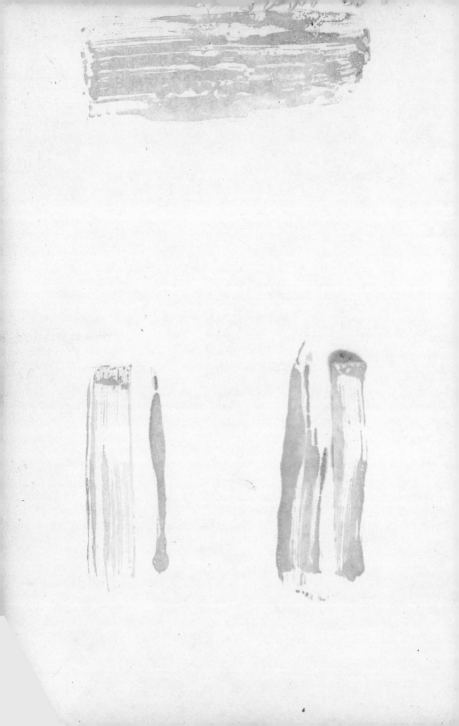